T0356452

LOUISIANA TECH'S
DAVE NITZ

THE VOICE OF THE BULLDOGS

CHRIS KENNEDY

THE
History
PRESS

Published by The History Press
An imprint of Arcadia Publishing
Charleston, SC
www.historypress.com

First published 2025

Manufactured in the United States

ISBN 9781467159203

Library of Congress Control Number: 2024950545

Notice: The information in this book is true and complete to the best of our knowledge. It is offered without guarantee on the part of the author or The History Press. The author and The History Press disclaim all liability in connection with the use of this book.

You gotta love it!
—Dave Nitz

CONTENTS

FOREWORD

The Hall of Fame broadcasting career of Dave Nitz happened because of you. It happened because of Dave, too, of course. This guy had the pipes and the know-how and a run few others could even dream of.

But hear me out a moment…

If a tree falls in the forest and no one hears it, does it make a sound? Maybe. Maybe not. I don't know either. But if a guy calls a ballgame on the radio and no one listens, that guy gets fired.

Dave called a lot of punch-outs, but he never got punched out himself. Because he was good and because you listened. You listened, for all those years.

I wonder why?

Because of Dave. Freeway Dave. On the road, then in a press box, then on your radio.

"Hello again everyone.…Glad you coulda joined us…"

The Nitzer. The voice of many lucky teams who had him mikeside, but mainly, the Voice of the Louisiana Tech Bulldogs.

This book is to share with you, as best as Dave can recall, how he got here. How *we* got here, him doing the broadcasting, you doing the listening. It was a journey we all made together. And you gotta love that.

Thanks to Chris for getting all this together. It ain't easy, making the words line up right.

Thanks to you for listening all those seasons, all those years—and for reading now.

But most of all, thanks to Dave for remembering. If you've loved you some Freeway Dave over the years, you'll love these stories. Shoot, some of them are even true.

Teddy Allen

INTRODUCTION

Fifty years is a long time for a person to work in a profession, let alone at the same workplace. It would seem that way for Dave Nitz, the Voice of the Bulldogs. He has broadcasted many games and made many friends during his time at Louisiana Tech University. The West Virginian made Ruston, Louisiana, his home and embraced the Bulldog spirit of determination, prevailing against the odds and loyalty. Like other Tech luminaries, he had chances to leave the university for opportunities elsewhere yet chose to stay.

Dave never expected to remain as long as he did at Louisiana Tech. His dream was to broadcast in the big leagues. While that didn't work out beyond a spring exhibition game, Dave has enjoyed his time at Tech and the fulfillment of a lifetime. The path he took that eventually led to him and his family planting their roots at Tech would not seem to indicate that

Dave Nitz baseball card, Louisiana Tech University. *From Louisiana Tech University Athletics.*

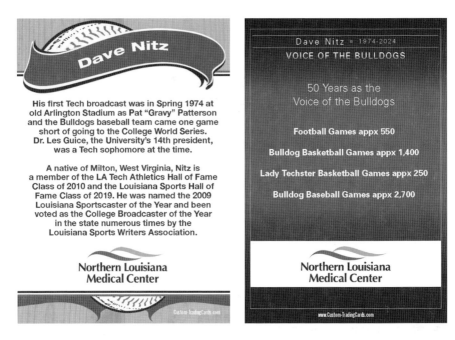

Dave Nitz baseball card, Louisiana Tech University. *From Louisiana Tech University Athletics.*

he was fated to grace the booth at countless Bulldog athletic events—yet he has done just that. For fifty years, the Bulldog faithful have listened to his familiar voice and recognized it for the professional and entertaining delivery of crucial game information. After all—

You gotta love it!!!

CHAPTER 1
WEST VIRGINIA

After Dave Nitz's fifty years in Louisiana, people might think that he is a Louisianian. While he considers it a fine home away from home, he hails from the place that John Denver sang about—"Country roads, take me home." Of course, there aren't any mountains where he's from, just hills. If you want to see mountains, go to the eastern part of the state. Dave was born at St. Mary's Hospital in Huntington, West Virginia, on July 10, 1942, some eight decades ago. It's like Mickey Mantle once said: "If I knew I was going to live this long, I'd have taken better care of myself." That's exactly the way he feels.

Dave grew up in a little town outside of Huntington called Milton. Sometimes, if he's talking to a fellow West Virginian, he calls it "Milton-on-the-Mud." Such a title would undoubtedly confuse outsiders, but it's really quite simple. The Mud River flows right through the town. After living in an apartment in Milton, the Nitzes moved to the Saunders Creek area, two miles from Milton. Dave will usually tell people something that Jeff Foxworthy might say: "You may be a redneck if directions to your house include 'turn off the paved road.'" That's exactly the way it was. It was a mile to US 60. That would seemingly qualify him as a redneck.

Another phrase he has used before that has stumped people is "frog strangler." Dave went into the office at one of the places he's worked and commented on the frog strangler going on outside. A frog strangler: a heavy rainstorm. The staff inside looked at him like he was speaking a foreign language.

Above: Dave's childhood home. *Photo by Tom Morris.*

Left: Downtown Milton, West Virginia, 1952. *From Dave Nitz.*

• • •

Nitz's father, Leon Nitz, worked at a place called the International Nickel Company—also known as INCO or the nickel plant. While growing up, Dave thought his dad would give him all the nickels he could want. He'd ask for them but soon found out it wasn't that kind of plant. It was a steel mill. In very labor-intensive working conditions, Mr. Nitz rolled sheet metal. Dave's mother, Wanda Nitz, was a homebody and somehow managed to put up with them. Dave was an only child. He speculates that perhaps after they had him, they didn't want anymore. What they had was just right—or perhaps more than enough.

Mrs. Nitz didn't want to drive anywhere. She wouldn't even go to the grocery store in Milton, two miles away. She was in her late forties when Leon finally convinced her to get a driver's license. That was an experience that Dave wouldn't wish on anyone, trying to teach her to drive. She was in her late forties. She learned so she could go to the grocery store on her own, but according to Dave, she just didn't want to drive.

Of course, Dave understood. He was also taught by his father. He was sixteen years old, practicing on a dirt road with a '49 Chevrolet. They were supposed to go down to the hard road (US 60) and come back. The Chevy was a standard shift, and Dave was struggling like crazy. By the time they got back to the house, his father was yelling at him. He was a perfectionist who thought you had to do everything right. Dave got out of the car and threw down the keys. "Dad, you can have the keys. I ain't never driving again!" Well, he eventually learned but could certainly see why his mother didn't want to.

Leon Nitz was a big man at six feet, two inches and 240 pounds. At the steel mill, he was one of four men who brought sheets of metal through a roller. One man on each corner. After it went through the roller, they flipped the metal and ran it through again. This went on until they got it to the size they wanted. That's all he did, all day. His wrists were gigantic. When he'd grab ahold of you, there was nothing you could do.

First Love

The first love of Dave's life was baseball. His father played and coached semipro baseball. There were teams from the factories at Huntington and some of the area small towns that played two or three times a week and doubleheaders on Sunday. At three or four years old, Dave started off as a bat boy. They didn't call Leon by his first name. It was "Nitz." When Dave heard them call for Nitz, he would start dragging the bat up to home plate while he was in the dugout. His mother didn't appreciate his early ball career. She always said, "You're going to get that boy hurt!" Once, he did get hit in the head; again, Dave wonders if that could be what's wrong with him. While shagging flies, or trying to, in batting practice, he slipped, fell and hit his head.

He had a big bump that nobody paid attention to, but he quickly figured out that sometimes, that's just the way it goes.

It didn't deter him. For some boys, love strikes like Cupid's arrow or a thunderbolt. For Dave, apparently, it was Newton's apple. He stayed around the game of baseball and started playing organized baseball when Milton finally got a Little League team. Dave was nine years old. The team's name was the Red Sox, so he naturally became a Ted Williams fan. He liked the Red Sox so much that he named one of his many dogs Dropo after the Red Sox first baseman Walt Dropo.

Dave played third base and occasionally pitched. He thought he'd like to be a catcher, so he tried the position during batting practice one day. It went okay until the batter swung the bat. Dave closed his eyes and got hit. That was the end of his catching career, and back to third base he went. Dave played Little League until he was twelve or thirteen. Then there was the Babe Ruth League. After that, he went to American Legion Baseball and high school baseball, all as a third baseman.

Dave attended school in Milton from grade school through high school, and he was fortunate enough to play baseball, basketball and football. Milton Elementary had a basketball team that played at a nearby skating rink.

Opposite: Leon and Wanda Nitz. *From Dave Nitz.*

Left: Five-year-old Dave. *From Dave Nitz.*

Below: The Milton Red Sox team picture, 1951; Dave is in the middle of the back row and his father, Leon, is the coach on the far right. *From Dave Nitz.*

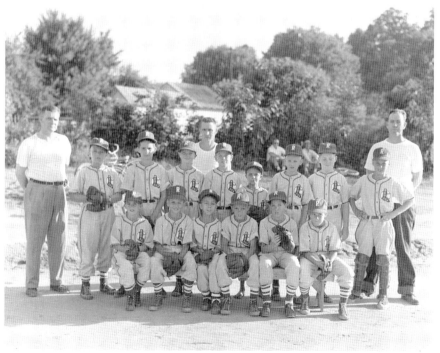

Milton's American Legion baseball team picture, 1961; Dave is on the right end of the back row, beside his father, Leon, one of the coaches. *From Dave Nitz.*

They put up some baskets in the rink, which was how Dave started playing in fifth grade. Playing on eight-foot baskets really helped him shooting-wise. To Dave, too many kids today try to throw it up at a regular ten-foot goal, but they're throwing the ball, not shooting it. He learned to shoot the ball at a relatively young age. His father put a basketball goal in their backyard shortly after. Mr. Nitz cut down a tree and mounted the goal and backboard to the pole fashioned from the tree. The only problem was that it was on the side of a hill. If the ball got away, it ended up going down the hill and into the creek, so he had to be quick to save it from such a fate.

Being an only child, Dave quickly learned the necessity of doing things himself. He came from a humble background. His father rode the INCO bus to the nickel plant. The Nitzes grew their own food, rarely traveled and lived in the country. Dave didn't have toys other than marbles. Aside from a couple friends, there were no other children for him to play with. This made the family visits to see his cousin Harry Vannoy and the vacation to the Smoky Mountains and Grand Ole Opry all the more exciting. Otherwise, traveling for the Nitz family consisted of attending Union Baptist Church outside of Milton. Dave quickly found out he didn't like vacation Bible school. He couldn't stand being cooped up, so much so that he ran back home. His mother, though she never spanked him, only had to tell him, "Wait until your dad comes home," to let him know he was in big trouble. While he had to make do with what little he had growing up, Dave's independent, take-action attitude would remain with him and greatly influence his ability to keep broadcasting schedules that few others could match.

Afterward, Dave went to junior high basketball. They had what was most likely the worst basketball team in Milton Junior High history his first year. They didn't win a single game. The next year, they came back, played JV basketball and lost only four or five games. Same guys, but perhaps a little more mature and learned in the game. One basketball coach in junior high made everyone shoot layups from the left side with the left hand. He said, "I don't care if you throw it into the Mud River. I want you to shoot the left side with the left hand."

Next was high school basketball. Dave started his junior and senior year and was fortunate enough to make the all-conference team his senior year. He had a pretty good year his junior year too, but he tended to be a bit one-dimensional. He could shoot, but the defense was a little lacking; he even led the conference in scoring. He had a situation where the coach would yell for him to shoot the ball. Well, if there was a guy closer to the goal who was open, he would always fling it to him, but the coach benched him one game. He said, "I want you to come over here and sit by me 'til you learn to shoot the ball—when you get the ball, when I want you to shoot." He got to play in the second half and scored 20 points. He learned quickly to take advantage of the opportunities he had because sitting on the bench was no fun. Shoot the ball when you get the ball. Lesson learned.

First Chance

Dave was good enough to earn a college basketball scholarship to Fairmont State in Fairmont, West Virginia, a small NAIA-affiliated school. He played there for one year but was always interested in radio. Even growing up on Saunders Creek, he'd listen to baseball games. His father was a Cincinnati Reds fan; Dave was a Pittsburgh Pirate fan. Mr. Nitz worked days, mostly, so Dave would listen to what was called the "mutual game of the day." Back then, there were a lot of day games in Major League Baseball. Dave remembered requesting *Sporting News*. They had an offer; for twenty-five cents, you could get a little book that showed you how to keep score. Dave got that book and kept score listening to Major League Baseball games on the radio. He put the scores on a piece of paper so that when his father came home from work, he had all the scores of the day games for him to see in his little score book. Mr. Nitz really liked reading about the games; it was something father and son could share. Again,

being an only child, Dave had to learn how to do things himself.

Keeping score was how Dave started with radio. He enjoyed listening to different broadcasters, particularly, as a Pirates fan, listening to Bob Prince and Jim Woods. They were on KDKA Pittsburgh. Whenever they played on the West Coast, they usually started at 11:00 p.m. Eastern time, so Dave had his little portable transistor radio underneath his pillow. Back then, there weren't a lot of televised games. The Nitz household didn't have a TV until 1952, when Dave was ten years old. Even then, they could only get one TV station, the one that played out of Huntington. Other than an occasional Cincinnati Reds game, there was no baseball on TV. Other than that, Dave just listened to baseball games and always thought, *Man, wouldn't it be great to be able to broadcast baseball at the Major League level?*

His first attempts at broadcasting were to narrate basketball games at the house by himself. Dave was a big fan of West Virginia University. He knew every player on the team. He'd shoot and say, "Jerry West just hit a jumper to win the game over Pitt!" and such. Of course, they were out in the country. No one could hear him, only the squirrels and rabbits running away from his dog Dropo. "Thank goodness!" says Dave about these early efforts.

His first real foray into radio was in high school. There was a sock hop every Friday night after a home football game. A disc jockey from one of the stations in Huntington came up, and he'd spin the records. There was Dave watching. That's what he did; he didn't think anything about the dancing

Opposite: A young Dave Nitz. *From Dave Nitz.*

Right: Dave Nitz, junior year basketball photograph, 1958–59. *From Dave Nitz.*

Below: The Milton Junior High School basketball team; Dave is on the right end of the back row. *From Dave Nitz.*

part. He just wanted to see what the disc jockey was doing, try to learn as much as he could and talk to the DJ. He got really interested in radio; when he went to Fairmont State, the fascination remained.

• • •

In those days, freshmen weren't eligible to play varsity basketball, so Dave played on the freshman team. When the varsity team played, the station WMMN, in Fairmont, broadcasted the game. He got to be very good friends with Frank Lee. He did the play-by-play and asked Dave to keep stats. Of course he would. Now he was traveling with the radio crew. He hung out at the radio station downtown in Fairmont as much as he could and became really interested in broadcasting. He began to think that this was what he wanted to do, although he still wanted to play basketball and baseball.

Dave stayed at Fairmont State for one more year. The next year, 1961, he learned that a new radio station, WSPZ, was going on the air in Spencer, West Virginia. Gordon Mims, the owner of the station, coincidentally had a farm right beside his grandfather's. Dave's grandfather knew Mims and took young Dave to meet him. He told Dave the usual. "Well, we're just putting this station on the air, and I don't know what's going to happen," and so forth. He said the station would go on live in September and that Dave should keep in touch. Dave kept going back to him every time he'd go see his grandfather, knocking on the door and saying, "Mr. Mims, are you ready to hire me? I still want to get into radio." He might have worn out his welcome.

Eventually, Mims must have finally gotten tired of being asked because he finally said, "Okay, we've hired a program director from Paintsville,* Kentucky. His name is Tom T. Hall." Hall was from Olive Hill, Kentucky, and of course, no one knew who Tom T. Hall was at the time. Dave was given a night shift as a disc jockey from 6:00 p.m. to 10:00 p.m. He had an all-request show taking requests for rock-and-roll music and called it *Big Dave's Night Beat.* He made forty dollars a week and five dollars extra if he cleaned up the station after signing off the air at night. Back then, there weren't many twenty-four-hour-a-day radio stations. He took the trash out— everything was wiped down and so forth so Tom T. would keep him around.

His first sports broadcast came about rather fortuitously. They were having a staff meeting in September '61. Tom T. Hall said, "We need

*Or Prestonsburg, Dave can't recall; they're close beside each other in Kentucky.

Right: Dave Nitz, senior year
basketball photograph, 1959–60.
From Dave Nitz.

Below: Milton High School football
juniors, 1958; Dave is number 32,
third from left, holding one end of
the football. *From Dave Nitz.*

to get involved in the community and do some high school football games. Does anybody have any experience?" He looked around the room and, of course, all the older guys, probably twenty-eight to thirty-two years old, said, "I don't know anything about sports."

Dave, however, raised his hand and said, "It's something I'd like to do one of these days. I'd like to be able to do play-by-play work as a career." Tom T. asked if he had experience. "No, not really. I don't have any experience; I just want to get started."

"Are—are you sure?" he asked. "Any of you other guys want to do this?"

They said, "No, let the young kid do it." Dave was nineteen years old. He was assigned the game that Friday night between Spencer High and Glenville High, two small schools in West Virginia.

Tom T. told him, "You're going to have to set up your own equipment. You're going to have to read the commercials aloud, no one else is going to help you, and you don't have a color guy. You're going to have to do it all yourself."

There he was, doing the first game by himself. Back then, they

Dave Nitz, senior year football, 1959. *From Dave Nitz.*

didn't have the two-way communication back to the station like they have now. They could hear him, but he couldn't hear the commercials or anything like that. That's when he started using a stopwatch. There weren't any telephones in the press box. Just a telephone for him to hook in his equipment. He went to a service station about a quarter mile from the school and called the station. He needed to know what time it was so he could set his stopwatch and know when to go start. To this day, Dave still uses his stopwatch, even though he can hear the commercials. He hits the stopwatch just out of habit. What if he can't hear the commercials? He'd be up a creek without a paddle. What if he can't hear when something goes wrong? Another tip he picked up involved spotting boards. Dave found some old pieces of ceiling tile at the radio station when the new station was built. They were lying in the corner, and he thought, *Man, this may make me some spotting boards*. He cut them into the size he wanted and used the lineup charts that he still uses. The idea for spotting

Nineteen-year-old Dave at WSPZ radio station in Spencer, West Virginia. *Photo by Tom Morris.*

boards is still in use today. Dave's been fooling people that long with them. He supposes he must have done an okay job since he's been doing it for so long, even though it's time to wrap it up.

Tom T. had the afternoon show. He would bring a guitar to the station and just open up the mike and start playing his guitar and singing. The manager came into the station one day and said, "Tom T., you've got to quit this singing. We're getting too many complaints about you singing on the air."

Tom said, "Well, that's something I want to do eventually."

The GM said, "Well, you're going to have to quit doing this on the air." Tom didn't. He kept on doing it, and finally the GM came in and said, "Tom T., I mean it, you're going to have to quit. This is no place for you to sing on the air and play your guitar. You're to play records and commercials." Well, maybe a few days or a week later, Dave came into the radio station one afternoon and saw Tom was loading up his car.

Dave called him Mr. Hall. "Mr. Hall, where are you going?"

He said, "I'm going to Nashville. The GM has just pissed me off. I'm leaving. I'm going to go make me some money in Nashville." Of course, the old WSPZ Dave thought, *Sure, you're going to make some money. You're going to make some money in Nashville. You're going to be a poor man pretty soon.* Tom T. proved everyone wrong. Most people know him for writing "Harper Valley PTA," sung by Jeannie C. Riley. He's been in Nashville ever since. Last time Dave saw him was in Shreveport where KWKH had a concert at the old Hirsch Coliseum. The GM, whom Dave had gotten to know, was Gene Dickerson. He told him the story about Tom T. Hall, and Dickerson gave him a backstage pass. Dave went to the concert and then went back afterward and talked to Tom T. They got on the bus and reminisced about their days at WSPZ at Spencer, West Virginia. Dave wanted to meet him again but never got the chance to. He was sad to hear of the musician's recent passing.

• • •

Dave stayed in Spencer for about five or six months. He decided he might need to go back to college, so he went to Beckley, West Virginia, where there was a junior college. It's been renamed since then, as a lot of places have. He stayed at a rooming house run by an old miner and his wife. The Beckley College basketball team was housed there also, and his roommate was a pretty good player named Larry Sumpter. He asked Larry if he should try out for the basketball team. Larry said, "I don't know, why don't you ask Coach Cook?" the head coach of the Beckley College basketball team. Dave told him about his time at Fairmont State when the coach asked about his background.

He said, "They're in the same conference as we are. You can work out with us, but you can't play because rules say you have to wait. But you can come out and practice with us on the scout squad and work out." This was in winter of 1961 at the start of the second semester. The conference had a rule where you had to wait thirty-six weeks when transferring to a school in the same conference to be eligible. Dave would have to wait until October to play in games.

In the meantime, he got a part-time job at WJLS in Beckley. One of the basketball players from New Jersey, who went by Joe Mary, told him he was leaving the station. He knew Dave was interested in radio and told him to go see the general manager at the radio station. Gene Morehouse, the GM, turned out to be the best contact Dave would ever have. Gene was named Sportscaster of the Year in the state of West Virginia probably a half-dozen times at least. In fact, he became the play-by-play guy at Marshall University and unfortunately was killed in the 1970 Marshall football team plane crash.

Dave was around the radio station a lot despite being part-time. He worked a lot of weekends and some nights. They carried the Cincinnati Reds baseball games. He could listen to a baseball game and hopefully try to get some pointers and do his homework at the same time. Gene took him to some football games that fall to broadcast basketball games after listening to a tape or two of Dave's. He also did high school sports. Dave was never on the air with him, but Gene would point out different things. Dave learned a lot of what would become kind of second nature, anything from prep work to arranging lineups

Dave holding one of his ceiling tiles, one of the trade secrets of broadcasting he picked up at WSPZ in Spencer, West Virginia. *Photo by Tom Morris.*

and so forth. Gene really took Dave by the hand and the ear, so to speak.

So there he was at Beckley College in October 1962, working with Gene Morehouse at WJLS while trying to finish his junior college degree in accounting. Coach Cook came to him and said, "Well, I watched you work out last winter, and we've got an opening. I'd like to go ahead and give you a scholarship if you'd like to play basketball here at Beckley." Dave said, "Well, coach, I appreciate it, but during the summer, they made me full-time at the radio station. I only have one year to play junior college basketball, and I don't think my college basketball career is going to go much further than maybe one year. I may get into a four-year school, but that's not going to be anything I would really be enthralled by. I'm going to have to turn you down."

NEW DIRECTION

On June 22, 1963, Dave married the love of his life, Marlene. They celebrated their fiftieth anniversary in June 2013. After completing his associate's degree in the spring of 1963, while working at WJLS, he got a call from WKOY in Bluefield, West Virginia. It was about fifty miles south of Beckley on the Virginia state line. Again, at first, he would be doing disc jockey work but also play-by-play. There were three high schools: Bluefield Beaver High School and Park Central High School on the West Virginia side and Graham High School on the Virginia side. Usually, Beaver played on Friday nights and Graham on Saturdays. If they both had home games, they were played at Mitchell Stadium. Park Central, an all-Black school, played on Thursdays. In addition to these games, Dave also covered Bluefield State College, essentially an all-Black school, on Saturdays. So, there were some times where he got three or four football games all in one weekend. Then he got into high school basketball and minor league baseball for the Bluefield Orioles.

The Orioles, a farm team of the Baltimore Orioles, was a member of the Appalachian League. Dave thought this was the beginning of the fulfillment of dreams he had long ago as a kid of broadcasting in the Major League. But he also saw an opportunity to play. He went to Billy Hunter, who would eventually become the manager of the Texas Rangers. He wanted to try out—back then, you could try out for short season A League or rookie teams. They let him try out as a pitcher. Looking back, Dave felt that he should have known he wasn't going to last too long because he was given the number 55. Players who had to wear a big number like that, even at spring training today, are usually not going to make the Major League play. So, he tried, pitched and was released. Hunter said, "Well, we need somebody who can really throw hard. You have a good knuckleball and curveball and all that, but you don't throw hard enough for us to keep you." Dave told him that he understood. "But the Pirates are looking for a pitcher over in Salem, Virginia, in our league, and they're coming in next week. I'll get in touch with their manager and see if you can get in and work the bullpen with those guys."

Dave happily said he'd keep it in mind. Sure enough, he got to throw in the bullpen for the manager. He said he could probably use Nitz, but Dave wanted to know what they would pay him because he was working full-time at the radio station in Bluefield and had just got married. It was going to be $200 a month. According to Dave, he did take accounting

The Nitz family, December 1961. *From Dave Nitz.*

and know a little about figures. He thought, *Well, I'm making $400 a month at the radio station and I'm getting to broadcast minor league baseball, and he wants to pay me $200 a month to pitch baseball. I think the better deal is to stick with radio. Maybe my future is a little bit brighter in radio than it is in pitching baseball because of my knuckleball.* He wasn't going to be a Wakefield or a Niekro. He said no but that he appreciated it.

Dave went back to Bluefield and asked Billy Hunter if he could throw batting practice. He was delighted to have Nitz back. He threw batting practice for every home game. He threw the entire practice, took a shower afterward and went to the booth to broadcast for the game.

• • •

Dave made a mistake one game in Johnson City, Tennessee. One of Bluefield's players had already hit two home runs that game. He hit a ball to left field, and Dave was right on top of it. It was a deep drive into left field, and he said, "It may be out of there—a home run for so-and-so! You can kiss that one goodbye." Then there was dead air, maybe thirty seconds—which you never want on the radio—while the left fielder leaned over the fence and made the catch. Dave had to say, "Well, it didn't quite get out of the reach of the left fielder. He made the catch." He bet there were a dozen people when he got back to Bluefield telling him things like, "Don't you know a home run when there's one hit?!"

At a game in Harlan, Kentucky, there was a shooting that occurred in or near the ballpark. A coal miner strike was going on, which was what caused the violent dispute. All Dave remembered is telling his radio engineer that they were getting out of there. They left as soon as they could when the game was finished.

CHAPTER 2

ODYSSEY

The next few years were among the most turbulent of Dave Nitz's life. He bounced around like he was in a pinball machine. After the Bluefield Oriole baseball season ended, he got a job at WMOA Radio in Marietta, Ohio. He was to be the sports director and news director. Marlene, Dave's wife, was pregnant with their first child, Jamie. Dave and his cousin Harry Vannoy were painting the house that the Nitzes renting. Marlene of course wasn't around for the painting because of the fumes. All of a sudden, they heard on a radio station that President John F. Kennedy had been shot. Dave knew he had to get off the stepladder and get to his radio station quickly. He was there all night long, taking calls, making reports. They carried NBC, which served as the national news angle, while Dave took calls and incorporated quotes from the mayor and others for the local reactions.

Dave didn't stay long at Marietta, only a few months. Turned out there was another guy who was doing play-by-play for high school and for Marietta College. Management said Dave would be able to do so as well. But that wasn't how he originally understood the arrangement and quickly determined that he would be a short time there.

Back to West Virginia it was. The Nitz family went downriver to Parkersburg. Jamie was born there on June 15, 1964, at Camden Clark Hospital. The radio station, WPAR, covered high school basketball games in Belpre, Ohio, across the Ohio River, and games at Parkersburg Catholic. In addition, Dave had a disc jockey show and a record hop at a skating rink in Belpre on Friday nights when there wasn't a basketball game. They paid

Lifestyles

Ruston Daily Leader

Sunday, June 23, 2013 • Page 1B

Submitted photos

The Nitzes celebrate Golden Anniversary

David and Marlene Nitz celebrated their 50th wedding anniversary June 22. The couple were married June 22, 1963, at Pea Ridge Methodist Church in Huntington, W. Va.

The couple currently reside in Haughton, where she works at Willis-Knighton Health Systems and he will begin his 38th year as the Voice of the Bulldogs for Louisiana Tech University in the fall.

They have three children and six grandchildren.

Dave and Marlene cutting the wedding cake, June 22, 1963. *From Dave Nitz.*

him twenty-five dollars a week to come over and do a record hop on the air. He thought he was rolling in the bucks now. After the record hop, he and Marlene would go to Shoney's for dinner, usually at 11:00 p.m. Dave stayed there for a little while and pitched for a semipro team in Parkersburg.

Well, that didn't last long either. Here they came back to Bluefield. Dave remained there for another couple of years. Jamie was about six months old when they came back. Dave broadcasted at WKOI again and pitched at batting practice for the Orioles once more. He brought Marlene and Jamie up to the press box for the first game. Dave likes to tell people that she watched her first baseball game when she was six months old, though she doesn't remember much for sure.

• • •

Dave always had what Merle Haggard sang about, "Ramblin' Fever." After his short return to Bluefield, he was off to Piqua, Ohio, outside of Dayton to WPTW, once again doing pretty much everything in radio: writing copy, doing disc jockey work, production, news and sports, including high school football and basketball. They covered Piqua Catholic and Piqua Central. Matter of fact, the station was solely elevator music. They couldn't even play Frank Sinatra—that was too "rock." After one year, however, Dave read an ad in *Broadcasting Magazine* for a job in Statesboro, Georgia, at WWNS.

GOING SOUTH

Dave wasn't sure about this but sent a tape to Don McDougald, the owner and general manager of WWNS. McDougald liked what Dave was doing and asked him to come down for their opening to call for Georgia Southern basketball and baseball, a NAIA school at the time. The Nitzes left Piqua one April evening. Of course, this is before there were many interstates. Dave drove through state highways and small roads down through the Smoky Mountains of Tennessee, leaving behind three inches of snow on the ground in Piqua. Compare that to what they found in Statesboro: the grass was green, flowers were blooming and the sun was shining. Dave told Marlene, "I don't know what they're going to offer, but I'm going to take it." He accepted the offer after the interview and meeting different coaches and other athletic officials. Jamie was about two years old at the time; everyone was all happy to leave the snow.

Dave had the morning show on WWNS. He signed on at 5:00 a.m. Again, no twenty-four-hour stations back then. So, he was up at 3:00 a.m. to get to the radio station, clearing the AP wire, turning the transmission on. They covered a bunch of farm shows and tobacco reports. Tobacco-growing country is from the Carolinas to Statesboro. Even back in West Virginia, they grew tobacco. From 5:00 a.m. to 9:00 a.m., Dave could be doing a little bit of everything. You name it: farm reports, news, weather, sports. He'd get off at 9:00 a.m., go back to the house, take an hour's nap, eat breakfast, go back to the station at noon and do the great show called *Swap, Buy, and Sell*. People called in with anything in the world to either sell, buy or swap. Dave did that every day from nine to 12:15 p.m. After that, it was the *Paul Harvey News*. Dave got off at 3:00 p.m. and came back for the sports show around 5:00–5:30 p.m. They covered Statesboro High School football and basketball.

While covering Statesboro High School football, Dave got to watch Ray Guy play. He was the punter and kicker for Tompson High School in the district and later served as the namesake for the top collegiate punter award. There was another little school, Southeast Bulloch High, that WWNS covered when there weren't any conflicts in schedules.

• • •

Dave started covering Georgia Southern basketball before they moved into the Hanner Fieldhouse. He actually started setting up in a crow's nest in the corner of the old basketball arena. The next year, they moved into Hanner Fieldhouse. Boy, did they think they were uptown. Dave was in Statesboro for three years before—you guessed it—before leaving again. He spent maybe half a year in Gallipolis, Ohio, at WJEH. It was a little closer to home, within fifty miles of Huntington. Almost-almost heaven you could say.

WJEH just didn't work out. Dave didn't enjoy it. He didn't enjoy the people working there. Something he would never forget was one of the things they had to talk about; the schedule of the ferry that transported people from Gallipolis to Point Pleasant, West Virginia. This was not long after the Silver Bridge disaster when the bridge collapsed in the Ohio River and killed forty-six people. A little ominous to say the least.

He called Don McDougald back at Statesboro, and McDougald was fine with Dave returning to WWNS. Dave and Marlene's oldest son, Jeff, was born on March 9, 1969, at Bulloch County Hospital in Statesboro. Georgia Southern was in the finals of the Division 2 Regional Basketball Tournament playing Mount Saint Mary's in Statesboro. If Georgia Southern had won that game, they would have gone to the national tournament in Evansville, Indiana. Dave tried cooking hamburgers for Jamie while Marlene and Jeff were in the hospital, but that didn't go very well.

• • •

Before long, he moved to Williamsburg, Virginia, to cover the William & Mary football and basketball team at WBCI Radio. He made a mistake on the air that he would never forget. You may be familiar with historic Colonial Williamsburg. Well, he misread it. He read "hysterical" Colonial Williamsburg. One thing's for sure, it was like that in the summertime because of all the traffic.

Of course, the football coach was Lou Holtz. Little did Dave know that in only a few years he would go to work at the same university (Louisiana Tech) at which Coach Holtz's son would coach decades later. How time flies.

He broadcasted his first bowl game when William & Mary played Toledo in the Tangerine Bowl. Toledo was among the best in the country. They had won twenty-two straight games and would go on to win a total of thirty-five straight games in 1971. William & Mary had won the Southern Conference Championship while Toledo had won the Mid-American Conference. Unfortunately, Toledo crushed them, 40–12.

Dave was driving down to Orlando for the bowl game with Harry, his cousin. He was a former football coach and was excited. They had spent the night in Statesboro with some old friends. They were going down Highway 301—again, before interstates were completed. The route led through Long County. Dave knew the history of the county from his Statesboro days. The state police had no jurisdiction in Ludovici. It was all the county sheriff. Nitz and Vannoy were going down a two-lane road, and Dave passed a guy going thirty-five, forty miles per hour. By the time he passed the other driver, Dave saw the blue lights behind him. The sheriff pulled him over, and Dave asked what he had done. He told him he passed on a double line. "Well, this guy was only going thirty-five, forty miles an hour and I was trying to get around him. I don't understand," Dave said.

"Well, you broke the law." A ticket was fifty, fifty-five dollars back then. Dave asked if he would send a bill or if he needed to write a check.

"No, we take cash." Dave thought to himself, *Uh-huh. I know about this place. I know where that cash is gonna go—in the pocket of this sheriff.* He and Harry came up with the amount and then toodled off down the road. When he got back, Dave sent a letter to the governor with a copy of the receipt. He hasn't

Harry Vannoy, cousin of Dave, in his football jersey for Salem College, senior year, 1963. *From Dave Nitz.*

33

gotten a reply from any governor of Georgia since 1970. Dave will advise anybody, if you're going through Southeast Georgia in Long County, make sure you mind your Ps and Qs. Don't do anything out of line.

• • •

When he first arrived at William & Mary, the basketball team played at Blow Gym. As Dave would describe it, it was a terrible place. But midway through the season or early part of December, they moved into the new arena, William & Mary Hall. The first game played there was against Dean Smith's North Carolina Tarheels. The arena wasn't completed. The windows weren't even in, and this was December. North Carolina had to park in the open end zone of the arena, which was kind of an open area where they eventually put bleachers. So, North Carolina parked there, running the exhaust outside. Dave can remember the white undershirts underneath their baby-blue jerseys. He was thankful he had a big coat on at midcourt where they broadcasted; at least the headset kept his ears warm a little! They had a thermometer down there; it read thirty-eight degrees at gametime. He doesn't remember the score, but was sure it was bad.

The station didn't cover any of the university's baseball broadcasts. Dave still had in the back of his mind this desire to do baseball. Well, he was there for three years. The last year, they decided to drop all sports at the radio station. He started looking around for a place where he could do sports. He talked to several stations: Binghamton, New York; Huntsville, Alabama; and Russellville, Arkansas. In the meantime, William & Mary decided to go ahead and cover the football games, but WTAR in Norfolk, Virginia, would carry the games. They let him do play-by-play, so for that last year, he did the William & Mary broadcast from the station in Norfolk.

• • •

Dave's youngest child, Jay, was born on June 15, 1971, at Williamsburg. Jamie was turning seven years old, and she was getting ready for her birthday party at the house. Marlene had everything ready, and kids were coming in. Marlene said, "I think I'm going to have to go to the hospital. I got something kicking me in the stomach." She got one of the neighborhood ladies to come in and finish up the birthday party while she went to the hospital. Jay was born that evening. To this day, Jamie says that Jay spoiled her seventh birthday party.

• • •

Dave got a call from Dan Hollingsworth, the GM in Ruston, Louisiana, who had an opening at KRUS. Of course, Dave didn't know anything about Ruston. Hardly knew where Louisiana was, let alone Ruston. He visited with them for several weeks before Hollingsworth decided that they weren't going to make a change after all. Laney James was doing play-by-play, and they were going to stick with him for another year. That was okay. He kept looking around and found a job in Russellville, Arkansas, at KARV in 1973.

This is where Dave ran into Gary McKenny. Gary's dad, Darrell McKinney, was the program director and chief engineer. He got to know Gary pretty well. They worked together doing several different things, including a livestock show in Olla, Arkansas, which is probably a story by itself.

Dave used to like to broadcast bowling matches. Whenever there was a strike, he'd say, "KAPOW!" Tom Morris, a friend of his who will be introduced later, used to ask him how many kapows in life he had lately. Another time, he broadcasted a golf tournament. He had his own golf cart that he broadcasted from. He tried tracking down the winner at the eighteenth hole at the end of the tournament. Apparently, the green is sacred

Dave Nitz, early 1970s. *From Dave Nitz.*

ground. Some of his friends quickly got him off green. Dave wanted to know what he was doing wrong. He had no idea he had sinned by trespassing on greens with a golf cart. One of the high school football games the station went to was in Atkins; they didn't have a place for broadcasting, so he had to set up on a small platform on a light tower.

The next spring, he got a call from Dan Hollingsworth in Ruston. "We've decided to make a change. Are you still interested?" he asked. Dave wanted to know what he would offer and how to get to Ruston, Louisiana. He came down one weekend to meet him at KRUS.

Top: Dave Nitz, student assistant Bill Thompson and Gary McKinney at Joe Aillet Stadium. *From Dave Nitz.*

Bottom: Gary McKinney and Dave Nitz at Joe Aillet Stadium. *From Dave Nitz.*

Hollingsworth hired Dave, telling him, "Part of the job you're going to do is calling Louisiana Tech football and basketball."

Dave asked, "What about baseball?"

Hollingsworth replied, "Well, we don't really do a lot of baseball." You can imagine Dave's disappointment. But he also had the opportunity to do play-by-play at Ruston High School. He recalls that he had help from students with stats: Pat Cobb and Randall Reeves. Both of them ended up going to Tech and working in the sports information office as statisticians. He also did some TV games on a tape-delayed basis for Ruston High after finishing the radio broadcast.

While helping Dave at Tech, Pat began to see himself announcing baseball games as well. *How hard can it be*, he thought. One day, Dave gave him the headset and let him have at it. It took no more than half an inning to make him realize he needed to go back to the chemistry lab and stick to premed. Pat credited Dave with helping him focus on his career path. He became an oncologist, and while work took him to Montana, he still listened to Dave's broadcasts and makes sure to visit him whenever he's in town.

FIRST YEAR IN RUSTON

Dave's first year broadcasting Louisiana Tech football culminated with the Pioneer Bowl, the university's second invitation to it over a three-year period. Tech played Central Michigan at Wichita Falls, Texas, for the NCAA Division II Championship but lost. From 1971 to 1975, Maxie Lambright and the Bulldogs had a 46-6 record. Weldon Walker was doing Dave's color. They drove the day before the game to Wichita Falls and spent the night right outside of it in Bowie, Texas. You know Dave; he's not going to find an expensive place to eat if he can possibly avoid it. Both he and Teddy Allen, another one of Dave's color commentators, are both kind of like that. If there are white tablecloths on the table, it's probably too expensive. They went to the Dairy Queen in Bowie to eat for that night. Dave didn't think much more about it. Later, on the air, he said, "Weldon, kind of an interesting ride from Ruston, Louisiana, to Wichita Falls."

Weldon said, "Yeah, the most interesting part was Bowie, Texas."

"Why is that?"

"The Dairy Queen. All we did was sit and watch the clock go around."

Dave Nitz and Pat Cobb at Joe Aillet Stadium. *From Dave Nitz.*

Dave didn't give up so easily on baseball. He went over to the ballpark to see Tech Coach Pat "Gravy" Patterson. He introduced himself, but of course, they still didn't get to do any of the regular season games.

Dave started at KRUS on April Fool's Day, April 1, 1974. Louisiana Tech got to the NCAA Baseball Tournament at Arlington Stadium that season. Dave talked to Dan Hollingsworth, who eventually said he could go to the game. He talked to Coach Patterson, and the coach told Dave to ride with the team. Tech won the first games against Texas Pan American and University of Texas but then lost the next two against Texas. They had come within one game of going to the College World Series in Omaha. That was before the super regionals.

About two weeks later, Dan came in and said, "We lost our production guy. He's going to Vicksburg to work at a radio station there. Do you know anyone who can do production, write copy?"

Dave said, "There's a guy from Russellville I got to know. He's really good. I think he'll do a good job on the air, does a good job writing." Dan wanted to know his name and for Dave to get in contact with him. So, he called Gary McKinney and told him about the job. He started around the first of May. Gary has always been a good friend. The Nitzes had him over for meals many times back then when he came to Ruston. He was a good broadcast partner too. Back then, the radio station was located above what is now Ponchatoulas restaurant. Elvis stopped and played music on the radio on his way to the Louisiana Hayride in Shreveport in earlier years. Gary and some of the guys would mess with the younger DJs and come up with stories that the room was haunted with ghosts to scare them at night, but Dave was too serious to join in the ghost stories. Little did he know that Louisiana Tech was the beginning of a new chapter in his life.

CHAPTER 3

LOUISIANA TECH, PART I

By now, you may be wondering why Dave moved around so much. Looking back on it, he wonders too sometimes. When they got to Ruston, he told Marlene not to worry. In about three years, they'd be back in West Virginia. That was the only way to advance in radio. You had to be on the move. The Nitzes could be back in West Virginia or Ohio— they both liked North Carolina. There were several other jobs that Dave interviewed for while in Ruston, but we'll get to that later.

At this time, besides KRUS, the only other station that carried Louisiana Tech athletics was KNOE FM in Monroe. Dave received calls from local journalists Ron White and Wiley Hilburn. They wanted to expand the Tech network. Dave had experience while at Georgia Southern in building such a network. Georgia Southern had hosted the Georgia Junior College Basketball Tournament, and he broadcasted the entire tournament while putting together a small network of stations in Georgia to cover it.

White and Hilburn didn't have much trouble talking him into it. Up to that point, he had been covering Ruston High School sports and Louisiana Tech football and basketball at KRUS. He had convinced Dan Hollingsworth to cover non-conference basketball games, but they weren't covering as much baseball as Dave wanted. White and Hilburn talked to Athletic Director Maxie Lambright, who arranged for him to work at the campus radio station KLPI and the ticket office with the late Flo Miskelly. Dave believed that Maxie was a great guy to work for

Dave Nitz at KRUS radio station in Ruston, Louisiana. *From Dave Nitz.*

because he didn't look on top of you and ask if you crossed all the Ts and dotted all the Is. He just gave you a job to do and expected you to do it. That's the way Dave like to work. If you don't think he can do the job, find somebody else. Shortly after, he went to work under Keith Prince as the assistant sports information director. His duties varied at that time from 1978 to 1979—anything from broadcasting and journalism to alumni events.

The athletic offices were in Memorial Gym. Keith Prince told Dave, "We don't have an office for you. We have an old broom closet over there beside mine. We'll clean that out and make you an office." Sure enough, his future office was full of brooms and mops that were cleaned out. Of course, the walls were very thin. Whoever answered the phone would peck on the wall and say, "You have a call on line one or two." By late 1982, the Thomas Assembly Center (the TAC) was built, which became their new home.

THE LOUISIANA TECH SPORTS NETWORK

It took a little time to develop the Louisiana Tech Sports Network, but before long, there were as many as sixteen stations going on the network. Dave would go out around the state and get stations to carry the games. They would figure out how much money he needed to spend or how much he had, so he knew how much to sell. He had to raise money to cover the costs for getting the games on the air—football, basketball and baseball. They weren't in the business of making money, but Dave did have to cover costs. He did a little bit of everything to achieve this—anything from sales to the ads, billing, collecting, formatting and play-by-play for several years.

KLPI

Dave was the KLPI campus radio advisor for fifteen years. KLPI was operated entirely by students. They weren't getting paid, of course. It was just a fun hobby. Dave had to put his foot down a little bit every once in awhile when the students would get a little wild with the music. He told them at staff meetings on Monday nights, "In the daytime, tone it down a little bit, and at night you can do basically what you want to do. If you guys keep doing this, I'm going to change this into Newstalk 89.1." That got their attention because they did not want to do that. They wanted to play their own music and continued to do so at night.

There were some good students who came through KLPI. Tony Taglavore, who was at KSLA in Shreveport, worked at KLPI. Barry Erwin, who was at WBRZ at the state capital in Baton Rouge, worked at KLPI. Sonja Bailes, KTBS Channel 3, was the last news director Dave had. Wiley Hilburn, who was on the faculty although Tech didn't have a broadcast journalism department, gave him leeway to grade their newscasts to give them a grade so they could get class credit. Most of the students were in engineering. They weren't interested in going on the air or going any further than just playing their own music while they were at KLPI.

Of course, Dave also did the sales and networking at the same time. They were running the sports network through KLPI. Dave sold it, made the format, did the billing and did the play-by-play. There were problems with people not showing up when the games were on the air—supposed to be on the air—so Dave took it on himself. He said to himself, "Okay, I'm going to give them—whoever we have, or whoever wants it—a scholarship. I'll pay for their tuition. That way, I'll have something over them." David Cobb, younger brother of Pat Cobb from Ruston High,

Opposite: Dave Nitz behind Grambling State University football coach Eddie Robinson (*sitting*) and Louisiana Tech University football coach Maxie Lambright, shaking Robinson's hand. *From Dave Nitz.*

Right: Dave Nitz arrives at Louisiana Tech University. *From Dave Nitz.*

Below: Dave Nitz and Tommy Spinks. Spinks was an outstanding wide receiver during the Terry Bradshaw era at Louisiana Tech University. *From Dave Nitz.*

started running the games and would do a halftime report, so Dave ended up paying his tuition. That way he knew that he had somebody there who could run the games every night, because they couldn't afford to miss any games.

• • •

There was an incident with the transmitter one week. They had to go through Purchasing to buy equipment, and they needed a part. Purchasing said, "Well, you have to put it out on bid."

Dave said, "Put it on bid?! We got a football game this Saturday."

"Sorry, we got to put it on bid."

"Okay, we just won't broadcast the game this Saturday."

"Well, I guess we can do it by emergency." They got the emergency equipment in, and KLPI got on the air for the game. Departments on campus are state funded; if they have leftover money at the end of the year, they have to turn it back in. Dave had an agency account, however, that allowed him some leeway so that he didn't have to turn anything back in and he could use the leftover money for things like equipment or getting more stations. Sometimes, he had to work around all the Xs and Os and all the red tape that you have to run through sometimes with state agencies. Nobody complained.

Top: Dave Nitz, 1979. *From Dave Nitz.*

Bottom: Dave Nitz and Ben Martin broadcasting a basketball game between USL and Arkansas State, 1979. *From Dave Nitz.*

When Dave started at KLPI, they were at about one hundred watts. After working for about two to three years with the FCC, they finally got the power up to four thousand watts. The channel was in Wyly Tower, the sixteen-story white building, the tallest on campus. They had a man who worked on the radio in Monroe for KNOE as the engineer. He'd do a Tech basketball game, working with one of the staff or TV people. They worked together for about three years getting the paperwork finished to get to four thousand watts. KLPI broadcasted a twenty-five, thirty-mile radius around the Ruston area because of this. After Dave left, they decided they didn't want the wattage, and the wattage was reduced. The studio was also moved to the Student Center. The first studio was off Gilman Street in a little doublewide trailer. All the equipment was in there. Dave was doing coaches' shows on cable TV. It originated from the studios of KLPI—for football and basketball. They would take phone calls for the show. Dave worked at the sports information office with Keith Prince in the morning before going to KLPI. He would come back to the sports information office and finish up the day there before going back to KLPI sometimes in the evening. It was often a hectic race between the two on any given day.

There was one student who did not turn out so well, at least at that time, though he hopefully turned it around. Students sometimes think they have to show that they can do what they want to sometimes. He had a show at two o'clock in the morning, and on one shift, he started cussing out his professor on the air. Somebody called and told Dave what was going on. He had to go down to the station, yank the student off the air, turn the station off the air and fire him. "Don't you step foot in this radio station ever again. You're out of here. I can't have that. You play your music; you don't do things like that on the air." There's always something that comes up in broadcasting and in life where you're not sure or problems you haven't dealt with. Dave has been broadcasting for a long time, sixty-plus years, but he admits he doesn't know everything. He was a little more structured than that because he had worked in commercial radio all his life. He was not going to put up with that kind of activity and did not believe that the university wanted that either.

Slow-Pitch Softball

When Dave came to Ruston, he organized a slow-pitch softball team called Sanitary Dairy. That was the team sponsor, Sanitary Dairy out of Minden,

Louisiana. This way, he could still get his fix in for pitching. It wasn't much, just a fun little hobby. They played all over North Louisiana, and Dave was able to get a lot of Tech athletes and former athletes to join in.

Tom Morris, who goes by "T-Mo" or "T-Bone," was a manager for the Tech basketball team at that time. He was from Hot Springs, Arkansas, so he and Dave shared a lot of similar interests from his time in Russellville. Dave tried using him for an interview one time for a basketball game against Mercer in Macon, Georgia. He needed someone for a guest interview, but T-Mo cut him off after two or three minutes. He said, "Dave, I got to go, I got work to do." He didn't know Dave needed him for ten minutes. It was a tight game at the half, however, so Dave understood that. It became something that they joked about later, like so many other stories.

Tom was the Sanitary Dairy's catcher while Dave was the pitcher, although Tom always said he was the better pitcher. He got his wish when he replaced Dave one time after a line drive bounced off the pitching rubber and knocked Dave out of commission for a while. They have been accused of being the best double play—for the other team. If Tom was on base and Dave hit a grounder, Dave wouldn't be able to run fast enough, so they would both get out. Dave, ever the competitor, maintains he wouldn't put it *quite* like that, but will admit that he wasn't *the* fastest person on the team.

COACH PATTERSON

Coach "Gravy" Patterson was a prankster. The baseball team was going up to Arkansas State on the bus early one morning when Gravy, at the front of the bus, got up. He said, "Okay, guys, McDonald's is on the left, Wendy's is on the right, and Burger King and Shoney's are down the street." Of course, everybody was asleep. They got up, looking around, about to get off the bus. Dave and his sons, Jeff and Jay, were on the bus. They got up with everyone else. Instead of the bustling metropolis that was expected, they were in the middle of nowhere on US 167 in Arkansas. "Where is it?" muttered some of the players.

"Haha, fooled you guys, didn't I?" Coach said. Funny guy.

Another time, Dave was working in the ticket office when Gravy wanted him to come to his office for a bit. "I've got the biggest fish you've ever seen. I was up on Lake D'Arbonne and got this big fish."

"Gravy, I don't eat fish that much. I don't even like it!" Coach insisted that Dave come see the fish. When he walked into the coach's office, there was a big can sitting in the middle of his desk.

"Just lift that can and look at that fish." It was a big old rattlesnake, dead, of course. Dave thought he was going to knock a wall down in that room getting out of there. Again, it was, "Haha, I got you, didn't I?"

Dave got him back. They were returning to Ruston from a game. A postseason tradition of Coach Patterson's was to have a cigar, but he never lit it. He'd just chew on it. Dave asked the bus driver for matches. He handed over the matches and some newspaper, which Dave wadded up, lit and fired up the cigar while Gravy was asleep. He promptly woke up, fighting and swinging. "Haha, I got YOU now!" Fortunately, Gravy could make jokes and take jokes. He was a sort of second dad to Dave, taking him in when he first came to Tech.

BEAT 'EM, BUST 'EM

Dave covered both men and women's basketball throughout the '70s and '80s in the heyday of Louisiana Tech basketball. It felt like covering a mini-NBA schedule going from one game to another. There were usually four games a week—two men and two women. Emmett Hendricks was the men's coach when he first got there. He loved the coach's little saying in the huddle: "Beat 'em, bust 'em—that's our custom!" Dave always told new basketball coaches the phrase, something they could say to the team.

SPOTTERS AND SHENANIGANS

When he first came to Ruston, Dave covered American Legion baseball games. He often hounded Jack Thigpen for the scores so he could announce them on the radio. Jack was a great high school and college basketball coach, and he helped Dave at Tech by doing color for basketball games. Dave actually moved next door to him. He was playing basketball one day in his yard and Dave came over to chat and play ball. He didn't expect much from Dave because he had also played basketball in college. Dave beat him in horse, and the two started up a friendship.

Dave had never had any help in radio before, so he got him to help do color. Later on, Jack also did stats during football for Dave. His help was greatly appreciated.

Sam Wilkinson, the Louisiana Tech athletic trainer, helped Dave tremendously during football games. He came to Louisiana Tech in 1977 from the Houston Astros. There were many times when Dave needed to know the status of players on the field but couldn't without having boots on the ground. They made up signals—if a player was hurt but was recovering well, Sam would touch the top of his hat. If he did not do that, Dave knew that the injury was more serious. That way, if parents were listening, they knew that their son was going to be okay. Other times, if Dave needed more time for a commercial break during basketball, he would motion for Sam to try to stretch out drills a little longer.

A lot of times, Dave roomed with Sam on the road. They often had wrestling matches where Sam claimed to be the champion. Maybe he was and maybe he wasn't. Dave let him think that a few times. They might have broken some furniture during these matches. Sam said Dave had the perfect face for radio. Sam said a lot of things, but so did Dave. It was always a fun time.

LAMAR, SOUTHLAND CONFERENCE TITLE AND CY YOUNG

In 1978, Louisiana Tech baseball was looking to win its second Southland Conference title in five years. All they had to do was beat Lamar one more time. The only problem was, they had been severely beaten by the Cardinals the day before. Mike Jeffcoat was a freshman on the team. Dave and the team were eating breakfast the morning before the game in Beaumont, Texas. Jeffcoat was a little cocky; he thought he could get anybody out. The team called him "Cy Young." He came over to Dave's table and said, "Nitzy, you ever called a no-hitter before?"

Dave looked at him and said, "Young man, you're crazy!" He had, in fact, never called a no-hitter.

"Well, get ready, you're gonna call one today!" Everyone was rather bummed out after how poorly the team had played the day before, so everyone thought Jeffcoat was just trying to lighten the mood. Not only did the freshman Jeffcoat throw a no-hitter, but Dale Holman also hit a home run toward the end of the game for the win. Once again, Dave was proven wrong. The Bulldogs went on to qualify for regional play at Arlington again but did not do as well as they did in 1974 when Dave broadcasted Tech baseball for the first time. Tech lost to Texas and Texas Pan American by wide margins.

KEITH THIBODEAUX

As you probably have noticed by now, being a broadcaster allows you to be behind the scenes, where you learn all kinds of interesting stories. Keith Thibodeaux was one of the best athletes Dave witnessed at Tech in the late '70s. In fact, according to Nitz, Thibodeaux was one of Tech's best athletes ever. He was the quarterback on the football team, played rec basketball and was the pitcher in baseball. Dave watched him dunk the ball in Memorial Gym many times. There wasn't much he couldn't do. Once, after Thibodeaux pitched a full game on a Sunday, Dave found him on the field running poles. That's when you run from home plate to the poles in the left field and right field and back to home plate. Dave was astonished. "Keith, what in the world?!"

Keith told him, "I just threw 150 pitches [I want to say in ten innings] and he has me running." Coach Patterson found out that he had been out late the night before the game. Coach couldn't have that. Keith got to pitch the game, but he also got to run poles afterward.

STATE FAIR GAME

Once upon a time, Louisiana Tech's biggest football rival was Northwestern State. Sure, there was old USL (ULL today) in Lafayette, but the Demons of Natchitoches always played Tech at the State Fair Game in Shreveport. Weldon Walker did Dave's color for those games. He worked in purchasing at Tech despite being a Northwestern State graduate. Dave was told Weldon was a great actor and speaker and found out that he was. There were a couple of times where he said the darndest things on the air. Tech was beating Northwestern State pretty good before the half one game. Dave looked over to Weldon and said, "It's a great first half for the Bulldogs."

Weldon replied, "I can't wait 'til halftime." Dave asked why that was. "They've got Oreo cookies and Twinkies in the press box and I gotta get me something to eat." Dave was at a loss for words. What could he say to that?

Another time, there was a Bulldog player injured on the field. Dave could see Weldon with his binoculars looking down that way, and asked, "Weldon, can you tell me who that is you're looking at, the player down on the field?" "No," he said, "But this gal in Section 103, boy, she's hot!" Dave thought, *Oh my gosh, I mean, there's no way I can come back because anything I'd say after that would be—nobody'd care.* They didn't rehearse anything. Teddy Allen can vouch for that. Things he or Weldon said just came off the top of their heads. No one else had any idea where they came from. Dave has been told that he takes broadcasting seriously, and he does, so maybe that's why he was at a loss for words.

NORTHEAST UNIVERSITY LOUISIANA FOOTBALL, 1979

The sports information director (SID) for Northeast Louisiana (now ULM), Bob Anderson, broke all the NCAA rules that he could. No one is supposed to cheer on press row. Well, he would often get up on a table and start cheering during the game if Northeast started doing well. But if they weren't doing well, you couldn't find him.

Northeast was not quite the same rival for Tech as Northwestern State or ULL, but there have been some points in time where the game was important. Like in 1979. It was the last game of, frankly, an awful football season. Larry Beightol was fired one game before the end of the season as head football coach of the Bulldogs, and Coach Patterson became the interim head coach. It was a hard-fought game that wound up with a Tech win by a last-second field goal by Keith Swilley in Joe Aillet Stadium. It preserved some pride for the battered Bulldog football team. Oddly enough, another Bulldog named Pat, Pat Collins, left the football staff not long after and created a powerhouse at Northeast.

NEW YORK, 1979

Once, in 1979, the Lady Techsters had just finished a tournament in Las Vegas and were going to Madison Square Garden for another tournament. This was five years after the Lady Techster basketball program was started. Jim Hawthorne was covering Centenary College sports at the time at KWKN. He couldn't make it to the men's Centenary–Long Island University game and asked if Dave could work for him since he was going to be in the area. This was a week after the Tech men beat Centenary.

Well, Dave flew up to New York City the day of the game. Only one runway was open at LaGuardia, so air traffic was backed up, and they got there late. Sam Wilkinson was with him. They frequently traveled together for sporting events. Dave told him to just take the bags to the hotel and that he'd be there late. He ran out, caught a cab and told the driver he needed to get to Long Island University for the basketball game. "When do you need to be there?" asked the cabbie.

Dave told him, "About fifteen minutes ago."

He said, "Okay, hold on." The road was already slick aside from the reckless driving of the cab driver, so he was glad to make it in one piece. "Here's the university. I don't know where the gym is."

Dave said, "That's fine, let me out." It was probably 7:00 p.m. by then. The game started at 8:00 p.m.

He started walking down the street and saw a little guy walking there. "Excuse me, sir, can you tell me where Long Island plays basketball?" he asked.

"Yeah, come with me," the man said. "I'm going to the game myself." Dave thought this was great. He introduced himself and asked him who he was.

"Lou Carnesecca, head coach at St. John's. I'm scouting the game tonight. Come with me, I know exactly where we're going."

Dave saw Centenary on the court right before tipoff. Nico Van Thyn, the SID at Centenary, had the radio equipment set up for. The only resource Dave had was a program, but he had seen Centenary play before. It was a tight game, and Centenary was beaten. The final score was in the 100s. Dave took no breaths until the game was over.

• • •

The next day, Dave broadcasted the Lady Techsters game at Madison Square Garden for their two-game tournament. Centenary was going up to Albany to play against Siena College on Saturday evening after the final game of the Lady Techsters. Nico was at the Lady Techsters game with Dave so they took a train up to Albany. Siena's SID picked them up at the train station. Dave just knew they would be late for the game. They walked in, and Centenary wasn't even there. They had gotten lost on the bus ride upstate. The game was supposed to tip off at 8:30 p.m., but the start time was thirty minutes late. Afterward, Dave just went to the team hotel and slept on the floor in Coaches Tommy Canterbury and Tommy Vardeman's room. The next day, they went back to New York and Centenary played St. John's. Nico and Dave took the subway to St. John's. It was dark on the ride over because most of the lights had been broken, maybe shot out. Dave was thinking about the worst that could happen, but nothing did. After the game, he took a cab to the Tech motel. Sure enough, Sam was there and had his bags waiting. That was one of the stranger weeks in Dave's broadcasting career.

FREEWAY DAVE

The birth of the legend of "Freeway" Dave came about in 1980. The Lady Techsters were playing UCLA in a tournament. Dave had never been to Southern California before, so of course he wanted to see it all. He rented a car and went to see all the sights. He spent so much time on "those infernal freeways" in LA traffic that Coach Leon Barmore called him Freeway Dave. He drove with Dave a couple of times but might have gotten worn out. He even wrote a song about it. Both Leon and Dave still have the lyrics if anyone ever feels like putting it to music. Dave played Coach Barmore in a one-on-one game at UCLA after practice. Dave decided to leave it up to the imagination who won.

They liked to have pickup games with Sam Wilkinson and Bob Ramsay. Ramsay did some color for Dave on basketball games. Coach Barmore likes to remind Dave of one time when he got Sam to set a pick on him. Coach Barmore thought Dave wasn't very good on defense. He would not have been the first person to notice this. Sam just about laid out Dave while Leon went on to make a layup.

Dave Nitz broadcasting a basketball game at Lafayette between Louisiana Tech University and USL, 1980. *From Dave Nitz.*

FIRST LADY TECHSTER CHAMPIONSHIP

The Lady Techsters' first national championship was secured in 1981, one year prior to the NCAA's first women's national tournament. The Lady Techsters won the Association for Intercollegiate Athletics for Women (AIAW) tournament, beating Tennessee's Lady Vols, 79–59, after going undefeated the entire season and racking up a 34-0 record. Held annually from 1972 to 1982, the AIAW women's basketball tournament was recognized as the Division I National Championship. The Lady Techsters competed in the AIAW tournament three times, winning the championship in their final appearance in 1981, a year when the Techsters were loaded with talent.

Junior All-American Pam Kelly provided the strength in the middle, along with freshmen Jancie Lawrence and Debra Rodman, giving Tech a 39–29 advantage in rebounds. Lawrence and Kelly would combine to score more than 30 points. Rodman's family was very talented in basketball; she, her sister Kim and brother Dennis had exceptional careers.

Angela Turner, the Lady Techster's junior guard, was named MVP of the tournament, contributing 16 points in the championship game. Freshman guard, Kim Mulkey, came off the bench to score 13 points, with a game-high seven assists.

A solid Lady Vol team, with a 25-6 record, could not get it done on the inside after the Lady Techsters forced them to take long jump shots. Six-foot, five-inch center Cindy Noble was held to only 8 points. Tech Coach Sonja Hogg indicated that the game plan was to control the middle and make Tennessee pursue an outside game. The plan worked perfectly, with the Techsters leading 40-28 at the half and going on to win by 20 points.

CHAMPIONSHIP WITNESSES AND MORE

In 1982, the Lady Techsters were headed to the first Final Four and Championship Game in the NCAA era after the 1981 AIAW National Championship win. The Lady Techsters were 35-1, with their only loss, late in the season, being to the Lady Monarchs of Old Dominion. The final four was held in Norfolk, Virginia, and included the Lady Vols of Tennessee, the Lady Wolves of Cheney State and the Maryland Terrapins, along with the Louisiana Tech Lady Techsters. That 1982 team was loaded with talent and included names that are etched in Lady Techsters' rich championship history. Pam Kelly and Angela Turner were both Kodak All-Americans. Pam was awarded the Wade Trophy, given to the best female basketball player in NCAA Division I. Also on the team were Janice Lawrence and Kim Mulkey, both of whom would win a gold medal on the 1984 Olympic team. Lawrence was named the Final Four MVP and Final Four All Tournament and also named to the All-Regional Team. The Techsters cruised past the Lady Vols in the semifinal game and defeated the Cheney State Lady Wolves to win the championship, 76–62.

One thing that Dave vividly remembers about that trip to Norfolk was that he, Sam Wilkinson and Coach Barmore were trying to find a place to eat. They got to a red light when they saw something that really shook them up. There were two lanes of traffic. In the lane to their left, a car pulled up behind the one right beside them. The driver got out of his car, walked up and shot the guy in the car beside them. Dave saw it. Of course, the guys tell it a different way. They say he couldn't have possibly witnessed it like that because everyone hit the floor and he was hiding underneath Coach Barmore.

An interesting fact about the 1982 NCAA National Championship Lady Techsters was that they did not receive their championship rings after winning the championship. In his "Lady Techsters to Receive National Championship Rings—35 Years Later," story on LA Tech's sports website, Malcom Butler quotes Coaches Barmore, Hogg and several of the players about why they did not receive championship rings. After thirty-five years, the Lady Techsters did finally receive their championship rings at a Legends Day Ceremony in Thomas Assembly Center on Louisiana Tech's campus in 2017. Coincidentally, the ceremony was held at halftime of a Lady Techster's basketball game. The opponent? None other than the Old Dominion Lady Monarchs, the only team to defeat the Lady Techsters in that 1982 season.

Grudge Match: Heartbreaking Loss in the 1983 NCAA Championship Game

The next season, heading into the 1983 NCAA Division I women's basketball tournament, the Lady Techsters had only one loss on the season—a 64–58 disappointment at home against the USC Trojans, or Women of Troy. Back before the 1982 championship, Kim Mulkey posted a then career-high 21 points while beating the Women of Troy in Ruston despite playing through the flu. That regular season loss was avenged in January 1983 with a 2-point win over USC in Los Angeles. The two were destined to meet again in the NCAA Championship game, just a few weeks later. USC's only regular season losses were to Louisiana Tech and Long Beach State.

Louisiana Tech hosted the Midwest Regionals of the tournament, taking down Middle Tennessee State in the first round by a score of 91–59. In the regional semifinals, the Techsters beat Auburn 81–54, and in the regional finals, Tech qualified for the Final Four by beating Texas, 72–58. USC participated in the West Regional, hosted in Los Angeles by UCLA and advanced by beating Northeast Louisiana 99–85 in the first round and beating Arizona State, 96–59, in the regional semifinals. USC then avenged its only other regular season loss by beating Long Beach State, 81–74, to advance to the Final Four.

The 1983 Final Four was held in Norfolk, Virginia, and included Louisiana Tech, USC, Old Dominion and Georgia. The semifinal games were rather lackluster, with defending national champion Louisiana Tech beating Old

Dominion by 16 points and USC taking down Georgia by 24 points. This set up a championship game between Louisiana Tech and USC—teams that had played each other twice in the regular season, with each winning one of those games.

The first half of the championship game was dominated by the Lady Techsters, with the Techsters leading by as many as 13 points and by 11 points at halftime. The second half proved to be a different story, however, as the Women of Troy used a full-court press to close the gap. With six seconds left, USC had a two-point lead. After a missed one-and-one free throw attempt by USC's star freshman, Cheryl Miller, the Lady Techsters grabbed the rebound and Kim Mulkey sprinted up court to take the final shot, but it was not to be. USC had won their first NCAA Women's Championship with a 69–67 win over Louisiana Tech. It was the conclusion of a rivalry between two of women's college basketball's top teams in the 1980s.

OTHER OFFERS

Dave had a couple of chances to leave Louisiana Tech before moving into the Thomas Assembly Center. WSYR in Syracuse, New York, placed what he always called a blind box ad in *Broadcasting Magazine*. It said major college play-by-play. Dave didn't know where it was; it didn't say. He just sent a tape and figured he probably wouldn't hear from anybody. Well, he did. The general manager at WSYR Syracuse called him. He really liked Dave's tape and résumé and wanted him to come for an interview. Dave thought the least he could do was go up and visit. He had never been there. In July 1982, he flew up from Louisiana, leaving behind ninety-degree weather. When he got off the plane in Syracuse, it was fifty-five degrees. He thought, *Oh brother, I don't know what I've gotten myself into with this cold weather.* It was the year before Syracuse moved to the Carrier Dome, so they were still playing their football games at Archbold Stadium. Dave always seemed to show up in places right before a new complex was built. He knew they had a AAA baseball team in Syracuse, the Chiefs, the Blue Jays' AAA team. He talked to the general manager, wanting to know if there was any possibility of doing minor league baseball. He told Dave they carried the New York Yankees on the radio and made a lot of money doing that. "I can't see us carrying the Blue Jays right now. Maybe somewhere down the road we can do it."

Dave said, "Man, that's something I'd really like to do. I'd like to get my foot into some more minor league baseball; that's still my first love." Well, he made the job tantalizing, at that point, in part because they were getting ready to move into new facilities in downtown Syracuse. Dave even got to have lunch with basketball coach Jim Boeheim, who showed him around the university.

He flew back and got a call on Tuesday from the manager of WSYR. "Well, we've listened to everybody's tapes, we've interviewed everybody and we're ready to offer you the job." Dave asked about the pay, which turned out to be $15,000 more than he was making at Tech. They would even move him up there and get Marlene a job.

"Here's the kicker," Dave said. "What about baseball?"

The manager said, "I just can't see us doing baseball right now. Maybe down the road we can do some minor-league baseball, I can't promise you that, but we're just making so much money off of the Yankees on the network. I feel like we need to stay with that right now." Dave thought that would be his chance to get into baseball. He told him he was going to have to turn him down. After a little silence, WSYR's manager said, "I don't know. I appreciate your honesty, but I don't understand your decision, turning this down." Dave replied, "I know, but I'm going to stay here in Ruston and maybe something else will come up another time." They had their goodbyes and moved on. Syracuse was pretty major; it was one of the original schools of the Big East, which was founded a few years prior. Hindsight's 20-20. A lot of people like Bob Costas and Marv Albert went through there on their way up to national TV and radio. Dave always says baseball keeps him in trouble because he loves it so much. He stuck to his guns, however, and remained in Ruston.

• • •

About two weeks later, Coach Patterson got a call from Hindman Wall, the athletic director at Tulane. He wanted to speak to Dave about being the play-by-play guy for Tulane and wanted permission to meet him. Coach Patterson saw nothing wrong with that. Dave was never sure—it looked to him like they wanted to get rid of him, but he never asked Coach Patterson about it. He had to be in New Orleans anyway for a Tech athletic event and met Wall down there. Wall offered Dave the job at Tulane doing football, basketball and baseball. They agreed on money and everything. "This sounds like a good deal for me, coming to New Orleans, a big-time city and a big-time university," Dave said. They shook hands, and each seemed pleased with the direction they were heading. Dave just had to give his two-week's notice, and it was all set.

On the way back to Ruston, Dave kept thinking, *Do I really want to move to New Orleans and bring my family down there?* Jamie was a junior or senior in high school, and Jeff and Jay were in junior high and elementary school. The longer he drove back to Ruston—maybe if it had been a short drive, he wouldn't have thought about it as much—but the longer he drove, the more he thought, *I just don't want to bring my family down here to New Orleans.* He got back to Ruston and called Hindman the next day. "I had a change of heart." Of course, he wanted to know what was wrong. After listening to Dave's concerns, he tried to tell Dave of all the other places he could live in the area. Dave could not be moved—he still had to turn him down.

He didn't think anything more about it until three or four weeks later when talking to M.L. Lagarde, who was at that time the sports information director at Tulane. "Dave, boy, you really screwed things up down here."

Dave asked, "What do you mean, M.L.?"

"You know, Hindman really wanted to hire you. He'd heard you do the Tech games on WWL in New Orleans, and you're the only person he talked to. He hadn't interviewed anybody else. He was set to hire you, and you turned him down."

Dave said, "Sorry, I just didn't feel comfortable with it. It just didn't feel like the right fit at the time."

M.L. replied, "Well, we had to hire some high school guy that was working over in Slidell to do the play-by-play."

Dave said, "Well, I hope everything turns out okay. I'm just going to stay here and do the Louisiana Tech games." It was probably a good thing too, looking back on it. Tulane became engulfed in several athletic scandals only a few years later and lost some of their sports for a time.

• • •

That winter, a job opened at Oklahoma City with the 89ers, the Texas Rangers' AAA baseball team. The Rangers had just acquired the franchise from the Philadelphia Phillies. Jim Weigel was the general manager. John Rooney had been doing the play-by-play with the 89ers and had just left to do the Louisville Redbirds in the same league. Dave couldn't remember how he found out about the opening, but he went to Oklahoma City for the interview. Jim hired him, and he went to work up there on the first of January 1983. He was working sales, doing media relations, doing the program, media guide and so forth.

The following fall, Jim Hawthorne called him. He was working at WJBO in Baton Rouge at the time. They had gotten the broadcast rights to do Grambling State football. Of course, Dave was interested. It would give him the opportunity to come down on the weekends. Jamie was a freshman at Tech so he could see her. He talked to the GM at OKC, and he was all right with it. Dave would leave on Friday, go down and do the Grambling State football game that one year. He took his son Jeff with him. He got his taste for the broadcasting side of football then. Dave had him doing stats for himself, which he enjoyed.

When Grambling State played South Carolina State, Jeff helped get the South Carolina State broadcast on the air. They were having some difficulty with their equipment. He knew a little more about the equipment than Dave. The South Carolina State guy said, "I probably need to take this little white boy with me back to South Carolina to be my engineer!" Jeff and Dave both appreciated the recognition.

CHAPTER 4
LOUISIANA TECH, PART II

Things have a way of working out. Dave was at the '83 Tech homecoming barbecue when Coach E.J. Lewis got a hold of him. He called Dave "Coach"—well, he called everyone Coach. He wanted to know if Dave was interested in coming back. "I don't know," he said.

"What would it take?" Coach Lewis asked.

"Money. It'll take money; that's the bottom line."

Satisfied with the answer, Lewis said, "Okay, that's all I need to know." Dave didn't think anything more about it.

A couple of weeks later, Dr. F.J. Taylor, president of the university, called him. He wanted to know when Dave could come down to discuss the job. Dave arranged to meet him at his house on the way to broadcast the Grambling and Southern Bayou Classic in New Orleans. When Dave got there, Dr. Taylor said, "We're not happy with how things are going right now. Can you do the basketball games starting next Monday?" Bob Ramsay was the play-by-play man when Dave was leaving the year before. Dave had no idea what was going on and never heard what the matter was.

"No," Dave said. "I think you need to give a guy a chance more than what you're doing right now. I don't want to undercut somebody. Whatever's happening, I don't know. But, if you're still interested when the basketball season is over, next spring, call me and we'll talk about it." He was later told that you don't tell Dr. Taylor no. President or not, it did not feel like the right thing to do, and Dave told him as much.

Dave Nitz, early '80s. *From Dave Nitz.*

Dave thought that was probably the end of that. He was probably not ever going back to Ruston or to Tech. Lo and behold, around late March, early April 1984, Dr. Taylor called him again. "We're ready to make a change. If you're willing to move back, we'll work with you on something." Perhaps the best way to describe President Taylor is that once he made up his mind on something, there was very little changing it; he was doggedly determined, progressive and controversial in much the same way as Raiders owner Al Davis or Cowboys owner Jerry Jones could be. Dave came back to do the Tech network again. He was on a nine-month deal. He could still go to Oklahoma City in the summer and broadcast the 89ers games, which he did for three years.

Dave has crossed a lot of bridges, both literally and figuratively, but ended up back in Ruston. He has been there since 1973, except for the 1983 Tech football and '83–'84 Tech basketball seasons. He recognizes that Louisiana Tech has been good to him.

BEATING JERRY RICE

The year that Dave came back to cover Louisiana Tech football was 1984 with head coach A.L. Williams. That is the year that Tech lost the Division 1 AA football title to Montana State. They played a team in the first round from Mississippi that had two future hall-of-famers: Quarterback Willie Totten and receiver Jerry Rice. Willie "Satellite" Totten teamed with Jerry "World" Rice to form the "Satellite Connection." Mississippi Valley State, college football's original "Greatest Show on Turf," was a national sensation. Their coach, Archie "Gunslinger" Cooley, came off the bus with a briefcase labeled "Gameplan" that was handcuffed to his wrist. Teddy Allen, Louisiana Tech University sportswriter and fellow broadcaster, indicated in the LA Tech sports site article "REWIND, Bulldogs vs. MVSU, Nov. 24, 1984" that defensive backs coach and former Bulldog great John Causey said, "I thought we were about to play the FBI." They were averaging about 60 points a game. No one thought that Tech would be the ones flipping the script on them. Dave can remember the band chanting, "We got our 60, where's yours!" Tech, considered as an underdog going into the game, won it 66–19. Rice even said in his autobiography, *Go Long! My Journey Beyond the Game and the Fame*, that he "cried like a baby after the game."

Dave had a crazy weekend when Tech made it to the Division I-AA football championship in '84. He and Jack Thigpen were covering a men's basketball game in Marshall while the championship was held in Charleston, South Carolina. Dave's father helped him get out of the pickle they found themselves in. He knew someone at INCO who was a private pilot. That man was a character. On the way to Charleston, he even let Dave pilot the airplane a few times. Louisiana Tech lost the game against Montana State 19–6. They immediately flew back to Marshall. Dave found out later that the pilot did not have a license to fly at night, yet there they were flying over the dimly lit mountains of West Virginia. They got back for the last game in a tournament hosted by Marshall before flying back to Ruston. From there, Jack and Dave drove to Houston to cover the Lady Techsters. They never missed a beat, but very few people outside of athletics knew of their skyward journey.

OKLAHOMA CITY 89ERS

There were good teams at Oklahoma City that made it to the playoffs all but once when Dave was there from 1983 to 1985. The only problem was, they could never beat Louisville in the playoffs. Dave split time with another broadcaster doing live TV every night there was a game. When one of them was on TV, the other one was on the radio.

Dave's father even came out to some of the games. He could stay as long as he wanted to since he was retired. Dave got him a folding chair behind the batting cage to watch him pitch batting practice, just like when Dave was with the Bluefield Orioles. He loved to watch BP before a game. The game was secondary to BP for him. He'd sit there with his Mail Pouch chewing tobacco—it was probably like heaven for him. This was during the last few years of his life. Dave's mother passed away in 1971 at only fifty-five years old. She had Alzheimer's. Dave would visit her on weekends to see her at the hospital in Huntington when he was in Williamsburg. She didn't remember him, only his father, because he saw her every day. Of Dave's three kids, Jamie knew her; Jeff and Jay were very young back then. But they knew his father. He was glad about that.

• • •

On July 4, 1985, they were playing before fifty-two to fifty-four thousand fans at Mile High Stadium against the Denver Zephyrs. It had become a contentious game as things started to wind down. Gene Duson, the Denver manager, was walking across the field heading back to the first base dugout after the game when he and the Oklahoma City catcher, Geno Petralli, had a few words. Petralli wound up decking him at home plate. Both teams fought all the way to the clubhouse, which was behind the right field fence. Dave Nitz and John Quinnelly usually did a wrap-up postgame show but instead broadcasted the fight. Dave walked back to the hotel with Dave Oliver, the 89ers manager, who had two broken ribs. John Elway was there—he and Steve Buechele, the third baseman, were roommates back at Stanford. Dave never forgot, Elway said, "I've seen a lot of games, I've seen a lot of fights. This is the worse I've ever seen."

• • •

Dave got to know a lot of the players at Oklahoma City. Steve Buechele was one of the best. He even came to a Tech basketball game in Los Angeles to visit with him. Dale Murray was another one. He had been pitching for the New York Yankees. Steinbrenner had hired him as a relief pitcher after they traded Goose Gossage to San Diego. Then, Dale got released. The Rangers picked him up nonetheless and paid him $40,000 to come pitch in Oklahoma City that summer. He and Dave hung out quite a bit. He was a country music fan like Dave. He'd always wear his jeans and his big buckle, cowboy boots and hat wherever they would go. He told Dave that season, "This is the last year I'm going to play. I've got a cattle ranch down in South Texas. My wife and kids are down there and I'm retiring from baseball." He was not young, being thirty-five years old. He hung it up that year and got out of baseball.

Dave also got to know some of the people in the Rangers organization. Tom Grieve was the director of player development. He had just retired from broadcasting Rangers games. He came to Oklahoma City quite often with his two boys, one of whom, Ben, also played in the MLB. They would be in the outfield shagging flies while Dave's two boys, Jeff and Jay, were bat boys. One would take the 89ers, the other the visiting team. Usually, Jeff had the home team. He would catch the balls that hit the screen as they were coming down. One time, he dropped one that had been thrown by pitcher Bobby Jones. Jones told him, "If it had been a cheeseburger, you wouldn't have dropped it!"

Jay would be on the visitor's side. Once, the 89ers were hosting Louisville. Jim Fregosi was the manager, and he liked to sit in a folding chair in front of the dugout. Jay decided that he would sit in the folding chair. Fregosi came out and told him, "Young man, you need to get up. That's my chair."

Jay shook his head, saying, "No, I'm not getting up."

Fregosi picked him up out of the chair and said, "You're out of it now!"

Another good friend was the late Mark Holtz, the longtime voice of the Rangers. Dave never forgot what he told him one time. They were sitting in the booth at Arlington. Holtz knew all the times that Dave had tried to get into Major League ball without success. He said, "Dave, I've heard you do games. You're good enough to do major league. You've got to think of one thing, though."

"What's that, Mark?"

"You're doing Division I football, basketball and baseball. You're doing minor-league baseball [with the Shreveport Captains by this time]. There are a thousand guys out there that would love to have that job. Just think about that." Sometimes the grass is not always greener on the other side, and even though Dave would have still liked to have been in Major League Baseball, the only time he ever got a chance was in spring training in 1983.

Dave was sitting in with Hank Greenwald. Ron Fairly was doing the San Francisco Giants color. The Giants and the A's were playing in Phoenix Municipal Stadium in an exhibition game. Ron had to leave early in the third inning. He had to fly somewhere. Hank asked Dave if he wanted to sit in with him for the rest of the game. "Don't have to ask me twice," Dave answered. He was there doing the color. Hank actually introduced him; he said, "Here's Dave Nitz, who does the Shreveport Captains games. He probably knows more about these players than I do, since he's been with them for so long." That's Dave's only claim to fame as far as Major League Baseball goes, one exhibition game.

KARL MALONE

Karl Malone and Dave Nitz had some big fun back in the day. When Karl first came to the Louisiana Tech campus, he was ineligible to play as a freshman. He would come up at noon to Memorial Gym, and they would play basketball with the coaches and some of the faculty. They were always kidding. Someone told Karl, "The reason why you got to be such a good player was you got to play with us old men!"

During the 1984–85 season, the one where Tech went as far as the Sweet 16 in March Madness, they had just won a game against Ball State and were driving to a tournament at Marshall. Karl was driving the van they rode to games. There were eighteen-wheelers passing them here and there. "One of these days, I'm going to own one of those eighteen-wheelers," he told Dave.

Dave said, "Uh-huh, right, sure." Well, just like Tom T. Hall, he proved him wrong. Maybe Dave should quit shooting down people's ideas. In fact, Karl owned a trucking firm for a while in Salt Lake City.

The 1985 NCAA Basketball Tournament was the pinnacle of Louisiana Tech men's basketball to date. They had a chance to avenge an earlier regular season loss against the University of Oklahoma in the Sweet 16. Along with Karl, Willie Simmons and Wayne Smith were some great ballplayers on the team. Andy Russo was the head coach. That was a heck of a ballclub. Probably one of the best teams that was ever assembled at Louisiana Tech as far as the era Dave was in. They had beaten Pittsburgh and Ohio State to get that far. It all came down to one final play in overtime against Oklahoma. Waymon Tisdale hit a last-second shot to beat them 86–84. If they had won that game and gone to the Elite 8, they would have matched up with Memphis State. Dave believed Tech would have matched up pretty well with Memphis that year. If they had beaten them, they could have gotten to the Final Four. Lots of ifs, but that was the closest Tech ever came to the Final Four. The Bulldogs lost a heartbreaker. That ball is still rolling around the rim at Reunion Arena in Dallas in Dave's sleep. It can't happen anymore since they tore it down. It was also Karl's last game at Tech.

• • •

Karl and Dave ran into each other a few more times after he went professional. Once, when Dave was in spring training with the Shreveport Captains minor-league team, he got a press pass and surprised Karl at a game between the Utah Jazz and Phoenix Suns in Phoenix. He had to do a TV interview for a few minutes before he came back and led Dave down the hall to the locker room. Dave looked like a little teddy bear with his arm around him. Dave wanted to get an interview with him for a radio show he was doing at KWKH in Shreveport later that night. Karl was always gracious whenever he wanted to do interviews with him. As soon as they came into the locker room, all the reporters saw them come in and started moving closer. "Hey guys, hold it a minute," said Karl. "I got somebody else I have to talk to first before I talk to you guys." They looked at each other and all but said, *Who's this country bumpkin? What's Karl wanting to talk to him for? Who's he?* They went to a corner in the locker room and talked for a while.

John Stockton gave them a hard time. "Why do you want to talk to Karl? I'm the guy that makes it go!"

1986 LOUISIANA TECH BASKETBALL

Another memorable and hectic stretch of broadcasts was in 1986. The men were playing in the NIT against Providence. Dave broadcasted that game before flying to Long Beach the next morning to broadcast two women's games. The men had beaten Providence, which meant that they were going to Madison Square Garden in the Final Four of the NIT. After the two women's games on Friday and Saturday, Dave flew back to New York City. They lost against Ohio State and won the consolation game against the University of Florida.

The next season, 1986–87, Tech played against the University of Washington in the Far West Basketball Classic in Portland, Oregon. Andy Russo was their coach, two years after leaving Tech. The Bulldogs came back to beat them by scoring on three straight possessions in the final thirty seconds to win 88–87. They faced Washington in the championship game. Tech was down late in the game. With those final thirty seconds left in the game, all Washington had to do was inbound the ball and keep it away from them, but they threw the ball away. The Bulldogs scored a three-pointer and then scored on back-to-back possessions for the comeback victory.

TRAPPED IN PRESCOTT, ARIZONA

In 1987, Coach Barmore and Dave went to see Karl Malone play in Phoenix. The Lady Techsters had a game in Northern Arizona University, so they thought they would get a chance to see Karl play the day before. There was an announcement at halftime that it was snowing outside during the game. Of course, people headed to the exits to see the snow. It never snows in Arizona. Leon asked Dave if they should leave. "Nah, we'll be all right," Dave said. They stayed and watched the entire game.

They were about halfway to Flagstaff on Interstate 15 when the snow started getting deeper on the side of the road. Up ahead were some blue lights. The state police asked if Dave had chains because that was the only way he could go any farther. "Well, I'm from West Virginia; we can drive anywhere."

"I don't care where you're from. If you don't have chains, you're not going any further," the state trooper said. Dave looked at the map he always carried, and they turned back to Prescott. By the time they found a motel, snow was about up to their ankles. They could hardly see in front of them or drive.

"Dave, we have got to head to that light!" exclaimed Coach Barmore. They had to wade through snow to get to their room. It was as if they were walking into a freezer when they got there. They turned the heat on in the room, but Dave's not sure if it ever got warm that night. The next morning, they trekked out of Prescott on the backroads through the snow up the mountains to get to Flagstaff. While Leon stayed with the team, Dave took a flight the next morning to Little Rock, Arkansas, to get to the men's basketball game against Arkansas State in Jonesboro, Arkansas. He called the Arizona state police to see if he could get down I-15. He could, but of course, he still had to have chains. Back through the mountains on those two-lane

Dave Nitz, mid-'80s. *From Dave Nitz.*

Top: Dan Newman, color commentator with Dave, Bennie Thornell and Dave Nitz. *From Dave Nitz.*

Bottom: Bennie Thornell, Teddy Allen, color commentator with Dave, Dave Nitz and Nick Brown, teacher and radio director of Bearcat Nation Network and KBNF 101.3 at Ruston High School, and host of the *Nick Brown Show* on Sportstalk 97.7. *Photo by Tom Morris.*

roads it was. Dave always said if he slid off the road there, they probably wouldn't find him until spring.

Dave made it to Phoenix, turned in his rental car and then went to Denny's to eat breakfast. Bennie Thornell, who did some color with Dave, picked him up at the airport at Little Rock, and they drove to Jonesboro. Dave did that game and then drove back to Ruston because he had another game on Monday in Houston.

A Game He Missed

There was one important time Dave missed a Louisiana Tech broadcast. The Lady Techsters were playing in Dallas against SMU. His son Jeff was on the 1986 Ruston Bearcat football team going to the Superdome for the state championship. Dave asked athletic director Paul Miller if he could get someone else to do the game so he could watch his son play. "I can't blame you; I would go too. If you can find somebody, do it." Dave had professional connections in the Dallas area who covered for him like he had for Jim Hawthorne for Centenary basketball and was able to see Jeff and the Bearcats beat Slidell in overtime.

Harassed by a "Blonde-Haired Woman"

Sometime in the late '80s, Dave was calling a men's basketball game in the TAC. He had a discussion on the air with Bill Cox as part of the pregame show. Bill was a Tech alumnus and athletic supporter. Little did Dave know the mayhem he had in store for him that game. As Dave was broadcasting on press row, a blonde-haired woman came and sat beside him. "Hello, Dave. I haven't seen you since New Orleans!"

Dave looked at her in shock. "New Orleans?!" By this time, the opening tip had just occurred. He was trying to keep up with the action when she began rubbing on his bald head. "Lady, you're going to have to leave here, I'm trying to work," he told her.

"Well, Dave, I'm trying to work also."

He said, "Ma'am, if you don't leave, I'm going to call security." By this time, Dave had his hand over the mike. At that point, she started laughing.

"Bill Cox, is that you?" What he had done was, with help, dressed himself as a woman, complete with makeup, heels and long fingernails. Buddy Davis, a longtime sportswriter in Ruston, had been sitting behind Dave the whole time and was probably taking note of everything until Bill revealed himself. It is unlikely that anyone in the stands even recognized him at first either.

SHREVEPORT CAPTAINS

Dave's last year with the Oklahoma City 89ers was in 1985. Taylor Moore, the owner of the Shreveport Captains, reached out to him about broadcasting their games and handling media relations. They also started the *Louisiana Tech Basketball Highlights* show in 1988 with CableVision in Shreveport. It was a televised post-game interview with the head coach. That was when Tommy Joe Eagles was at Tech. The Captains were the AA team for the San Francisco Giants. The new Fairgrounds Stadium was nearly complete. Moore was looking to build up the franchise, and Dave was a part of his plan. Dave wasn't sure about it at first. He explained to Taylor his arrangement between Oklahoma City and Louisiana Tech. He didn't know if it would be amenable to Taylor. "Well, I tell, you, I'll make a deal. You come work for me during the baseball season, and I'll let you loose after. You can do Louisiana Tech football and basketball at that time and do whatever baseball you can do for them and come back in April and work through the first of September for me." The Captains had a lot going for them, and they were closer to home. Dave even moved to Shreveport in 1991 and worked there full-time. He stayed there for fourteen years and watched them win three Texas League championships in 1990, '91 and '95 until they were sold to a group and left town.

Taylor was much like Coach Lambright at Louisiana Tech. They were the kind of guys who would give you a job to do and expect you to do it. They didn't look over your shoulders to make sure you crossed all the Ts and dotted all the Is. When Dave first got there, he asked Taylor how he wanted things done. He said, "You're the radio guy. You know more about this than I do. The only thing I want from you is to make sure that every night when I tune in to the ballgame that the game is on and you're there to do it. I'm not going to tell you how to do your job; I'm not going to ever critique you because I know you know best. I just want to make sure that we're never going to have any hiccups. You do it the way you want to do it." Dave gained

Right: Dave Nitz broadcasting a basketball game in the '80s. *From Dave Nitz.*

Below: *First row*: O.K. "Buddy" Davis, Ruston, LA sportswriter; Mason Ellenburger, Learfield's LA Tech Sports Properties GM; Teddy Allen; and Benny Thornell; *second row*: Dave Nitz and Max Causey, former Louisiana Tech quarterback and sideline reporter and current NFL on-field official. Snapdragon Stadium, San Diego, California, Poinsettia Bowl 2011. *From Dave Nitz.*

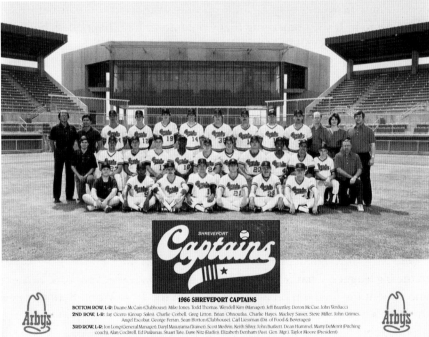

1986 SHREVEPORT CAPTAINS

BOTTOM ROW, L-R: Duane McCain (Clubhouse), Mike Jones, Todd Thomas, Wendell Kim (Manager), Jeff Brantley, Deron McCue, John Verducci
2ND ROW, L-R: Jay Ciceto (Group Sales), Charlie Corbell, Greg Litton, Brian Ohnoutka, Charlie Hayes, Mackey Sasser, Steve Miller, John Grimes, Angel Escobar, George Ferran, Sean Horton (Clubhouse), Carl Liessman (Dir. of Food & Beverages)
3RD ROW, L-R: Jon Long (General Manager), Daryl Masuyama (Trainer), Scott Medvin, Keith Silver, John Burkett, Dean Hummel, Marty DeMerrit (Pitching coach), Alan Cockrell, Ed Puskunas, Stuart Tate, Dave Nitz (Radio), Elizabeth Denham (Asst. Gen. Mgr.), Taylor Moore (President)

Top: Chris Weego and Dave Nitz before a basketball game between Louisiana Tech University and the University of Arkansas in December 2002. *From Dave Nitz.*

Bottom: The 1986 Shreveport captains; Dave Nitz is third from right on the back row. *From Dave Nitz.*

72

his trust from the start; toward the end of Dave's time in Shreveport, Taylor would let Dave go and negotiate the contracts with the radio station for the broadcast. He was one of the best people Dave worked for. To this day, they are still friends.

• • •

Dave had some help broadcasting games when Dale Holmon did some color for him. Dale was the former Tech baseball player who hit the home run in Mike Jeffcoat's no-hitter conference title game against Lamar. He fooled Dave on a silly story one time. He was telling Dave about his experience playing Mexican League baseball. One of the fields was not very good. The outfield fence and the boards at the bottom were rotten or missing, and there were houses behind the field. He said that he noticed after batting practice one time that farm animals ran onto the field through those holes. One game, he was playing right field when a ball was hit into deep center field and a hog came up and swallowed the ball before he could get to it. It was something that would never have happened, but here was Dave trying to call the Captains game and trying to listen to his story. Dale had Dave hooked. "Really?! What happened?" He said the batter ran to home plate, the umpires didn't know what to do, and the managers ran onto the field arguing about whether it should be a ground rule double or an inside of the park home run. He said that he couldn't speak their Spanish and had no idea what to tell them. Finally, they announced that since the ball was so deep into right center, they would call it an "inside the porker." That cracked up Dave. He could hardly keep it together in the middle of the Captains' broadcast.

• • •

There were many great players who came through the Captains and played in the big leagues. Charlie Hayes, who ended up with the New York Yankees and caught the final out on a foul ball to win the 1996 World Series, comes to Dave's mind. They nicknamed him "Scruggler." He had difficulty pronouncing his Ts and would say scruggle so often while describing a problem he was having that he became known as Scruggler.

Marvin Benard was a great story. He was drafted in the fiftieth round in 1992 by the Giants. Dave always says that if you're that low of a draft pick, you're going to have to prove every day that you can play. That's just the way it operates in baseball. Dave didn't know him at the time, but during that spring training, Marvin was hitting the ball like crazy. Dave was visiting with some of the Giants folks and said, "Man, this guy, Marvin Benard, can really swing the bat!"

They said, "Yeah, he's Class A ball, but I don't think he can play at AA."

Dave said, "Well, I don't know. What I'm seeing is pretty good." They eventually sent him to AA, and he ended up on a twenty-two-game hitting streak when he first came to Shreveport and hit about .330, .340 that year. After that, he went to Phoenix to the AAA team. Dave was watching him killing the ball in spring training there. He told Jack Hyde, the director of player development with the Giants, "Marvin's having a really great spring training."

Jack said, "Yeah, but we're probably going to send him down to AA. I don't think he can make the AAA team." He eventually did and had another great year there before going to the big leagues.

The player whom Dave continued to praise would accuse him of something taboo in baseball. While at spring training in Scottsdale, Arizona, with the Giants, he wanted to interview some of the guys who came through Shreveport. Of course, Marvin said, "Hey, don't talk to that guy. Nitzy will jinx you!" He had done an interview with Marvin when he had that big hit streak. That day, he ended the hit streak, and he blamed Dave for it.

Calvin Murray was one of the best guys that ever put on a Captains uniform, not only as a player but also as a person. A lot of these guys sent back from the AAA and AA have a little bit of a sour taste in their mouth. Dave understood that because you get to AAA, and you're only one step away from the Bigs. Murray, however, came back to Shreveport and had the biggest smile. He was happy to be there. He was ready to play baseball and never missed a lick.

There was a pitcher, Larry Carter, called LC. He was a fellow West Virginian. For some reason, the team always had fights with Tulsa and Jackson, but mainly Tulsa. One reason may have been because they played each other so many times. In the 1989–90 season, a fight broke out between the two teams. There were closed-circuit TVs throughout Fairgrounds Field and TVs all over the clubhouse. He pitched the first five or six innings and was down in the clubhouse taking a shower and changing into street clothes. He saw the fight and saw Walt "No-Neck" Williams, the Tulsa pitching coach, get ahold of Shreveport's pitching coach, Steve Cline, wrestling him to the ground. LC came out of the clubhouse, went out on the field in his street clothes and cold clocked No-Neck Williams. Knocked a couple of teeth out. Afterward, Dave said, "Man, it looks like you've been in a couple of these fights before."

LC said, "Yeah, back home in West Virginia, we had some bar fights. This was nothing, just nothing at all." He was last with the Kansas City Royals as a coach in 2022. Quite a competitor, as Dave remembers.

Ron Wotus was one of the managers Dave remembers well. He levied fines, lots of fines, against players when they didn't do something correctly, such as not wearing their uniform right. Jacob Cruz always made the comment, "I just as well may give my paycheck to Ron Wotus because it seems like every time I'm around I'm always getting fined." Ron would take the fine money and give it to the Boys and Girls Club across the street from Fairgrounds Field. It didn't go into his pocket. He retired from the Giants in 2021.

Marty DeMerritt was an interesting pitching coach; they called him "the Dogster." He was a big fan of Hulk Hogan. He lived in the clubhouse, and he had a bed and big pictures of Hulk Hogan all over the clubhouse and in the manager's room. There was a rain delay at Wichita one time, and he came up to the booth. He wanted to fill in some time while they were waiting for the game to resume. He got on air and said, "All you young ladies back in Shreveport who may be listening—we'll be back in town in a couple days. You can meet me out there at the Fair Grounds, and we'll do some roller skating." That was just off the top of his head. He loved to roller skate. Another time, Dave was interviewing a player in Jackson behind the batting cage. Marty came up behind him while he was on the air and got him in a big bear hug, lifting him high in the air while he was trying to do an interview. Of course, that was the end of that interview.

Bill Robinson, who played on the Pittsburgh Pirates 1979 World Series championship team, was a manager who was hard to get along with for Dave. He was handling media relations, and all three TV stations in Shreveport were doing interviews with players and coaches. They wanted a live shot with Bill, so Dave wanted to know where he wanted to do the live shot. At first, it was in the dugout. They had the cables ready, but then five minutes before, Bill said no, he wanted to do it in front of the beer garden. It was challenging to move at the last minute when the TV crew was already set up. There's always a little delay when one can hear the director and is waiting for the host to be ready for the live shot, but he didn't want to wait for that.

One occasion in 1988 left a mark on Dave. He was in the middle of a post-game interview after the Captains clinched the Eastern Division title when he was smashed in the face with shaving cream pie. Two players had already been smashed earlier that season. Mike Benjamin, the player he was interviewing, didn't even react. Dave's first thought was to wonder if he was still on the air. He was completely covered. His earpiece and only communication with the control room was gone so he just kept going. A similar occurrence happened with the Oklahoma City 89ers. He was taping radio interviews when Ricky Wright doused him with water. Between Dave and the tape recorder, they were soaked.

J.J. Lewis was the clubhouse manager. He had been a student at Louisiana Tech in the early '90s and was the team manager for basketball and baseball. Dave had gotten the impression that Lewis was in trouble of losing his scholarship at Tech. He also knew, however, that Taylor Moore was looking for a clubhouse manager. The timing seemed perfect. He mentioned it to J.J. and joined the Captains. They helped each other out. Occasionally, he helped Dave carry radio equipment around at Tech, and with the Captains, Dave used him to get players and coaches for interviews.

• • •

The first championship the Captains won was against San Antonio in 1990. The next year, they beat El Paso. Unfortunately, Dave missed both of those championships because he had to go back to Tech for the beginning of the football season. They missed the three-peat by being dominated by Wichita. For the last game in the series, the Captains were at Wichita, and they scored five or six runs in the first inning. Taylor Moore was with Dave in the press box. He looked back, and Taylor was on the phone with the airline, making his reservation to get back to Shreveport the next day. Dave said to him after, "The game's not over!"

He said, "Yeah, the game's over. Wichita's gonna win this thing, and we're heading home tomorrow." The best year the Captains had was the last championship season in 1995. They never left first place from the first game in April that season and beat Midland for the championship.

The years 1994 and 1995 were an interesting time for the Captains. Everyone was in the clubhouse when the Captains clinched a spot in the 1994 playoffs. In the background, on the TVs, OJ Simpson's white Ford Bronco chase was playing while everyone celebrated the game. At the start of the 1995 championship season, Dave was at Don and Charlie's Steakhouse in Scottsdale, Arizona, with Scott Ferrell during spring training. Scott was a Shreveport sportswriter who covered the Captains. Don and Charlie's was a legendary baseball establishment. Lots of celebrities of the game went there.

They had Bud Selig, the acting MLB commissioner, walk by their table. This was in the middle of the 1994–95 strike. Scott said, "There goes the man who's trying to kill baseball." Dave couldn't tell if Selig took any notice of it, but he at least got a good laugh out of that one.

There was an independent team, the Shreveport Sports. Once, manager Terry Bevington got into an argument with the second base umpire when he called one of the players out. While arguing that he was safe, Terry picked up the base and threw it away. The umpire walked away from him toward the left field fence, Terry following him all the way. Needless to say, Terry was out of the game. He told Dave later, however, that if the umpire had left the stadium, he would have followed him out.

• • •

Dave stayed with the Captains for a few years until a new general manager came in. They wanted him to stay as public address announcer, but they would hire someone else for radio. He found out it was a young kid who would do it for twenty-five dollars a game. That was understandable. A kid's gonna take it. Dave was in that same situation one time and would have done the same thing. He told them he was out of there.

One of the memories that is seared in the memory of fans who came to Fairgrounds Field was the little ice cream cups with different logos of Major League teams on it. When the Captains left Shreveport, they went to Frisco, Texas, where they could sell lots of tickets at higher prices. They moved to a high-rent neighborhood, so to speak. That's just the landscape in sports now. You stay around, you lose money, and all of a sudden, you've got to find a place to land the plane.

After baseball left Shreveport, Fairgrounds Field went to pot. The city built it on bond, and it was a nice facility. It was the mecca of minor-league baseball when it was built, one of the best in the country. People really admired it. Taylor Moore told Dave one time that they had better ask him about it. "There's so much concrete and steel in the ground. We made it to last forever." The city never kept it up. The ceiling tiles in the offices and press box are crumbling, falling down. Animals have taken over inside. Homeless people break in, knock down the outfield fence, knock out parts of the press box and skybox and sleep underneath it at night. It's awful. Last time Dave was there was 2008, and it was bad then. One can imagine how bad it is now. When Taylor Moore owned it, it was immaculate. He hired people to maintain the grounds. People wanted to go there. Before

Fairgrounds Field, the Captains were at an old stadium between Murphy and I-20 in Shreveport, which is hardly in existence either. Now, you can ride by on I-20 and probably think, oh, gosh. Knowing how it used to be and how it is now, Dave could just cry—seeing the weeds growing up in the seats and on the field. Now they're going to tear it down. Lots of luck. They're going to spend millions of dollars to tear it down. That is one of his biggest disappointments in pro baseball.

CHAPTER 5

A CAREER FULFILLED

After leaving Shreveport, Dave went down to work for the Louisiana Network as an affiliate relations director. He covered the new Baton Rouge Blue Marlins independent minor-league baseball team in 2001. People may not remember that very well because it only lasted for one year. The team didn't have enough uniforms for everybody. The player who pitched the previous night, so to speak, gave his uniform to the guy who was going to pitch that night or to some guy who didn't have a uniform. So, every night, Dave had to go down to the locker room and find out which numbers everybody wore before he could give the numbers to the PA guy and use for himself.

If there was radio for the other team, he had to take care of that too. The press boxes for the home and away team were so close that you could throw wadded-up paper balls at each other. That's just what he did with his friend Charlie Chitworth, the broadcaster of the Tyler Roughnecks. They were a good ballclub. Baton Rouge won the All-American Association championship by beating the Fort Worth Cats in its one-year existence.

SCAREDY-CAT

Dave had an offer to do some LSU baseball but he just couldn't do it. Jim Hawthorn, when Dave was working in Baton Rouge, wanted him to do the

Dave interviewing Willie McCovey, San Francisco Giants Hall of Famer, at Fairgrounds Stadium, 1986. *From Dave Nitz.*

weekend games and do a lot of the play-by-play to give him a rest. Dave would always come up with an excuse. He thought to myself, *I do an LSU game against maybe Mississippi State or Alabama; what if somebody hits a home run for the other team and I say, "Ya gotta love it!?" I'd get fired. They'd kill me!* People would say Dave was crazy. No doubt LSU is a great place to be, but he just couldn't see himself doing LSU baseball or really any LSU sports. LSU people might hold that against him, but it is what it is.

CAMPBELL UNIVERSITY

In 2002, Dave received a call from an old friend. Stan Williamson, a former Tech basketball player, was the athletic director at Campbell University in Buies Creek, North Carolina. Stan said, "I'd love to hire you. I don't know if I can afford you or not, but can you come over for a visit?" His wife, former

Lady Techster Debbie Primeaux, picked Dave up at the airport in Raleigh and drove him over to the campus. Stan gave Dave a tour of the university, and he visited with the coaches and saw the plans for a new arena, like he had for so many other places. The money was not what he was making at Tech. He really appreciated the trip and seeing what they had. They had a niche in North Carolina and were hardworking, but Dave didn't go there.

Later, when he became the athletic director at the University of West Alabama, Stan asked if Dave had any young broadcasters looking to get into college sports for him to see. Dave emailed him back a list of people and said, "I guess that means I'm out of consideration, because you mentioned young!"

He said, "I ain't trying to hire you again. I got enough flak from the Tech people last time that you and I talked. I'm not ever going down that road again." Louisiana Tech has some of the most loyal fans when it comes to their favorites, as Stan encountered.

BEATING ALABAMA TWICE

Louisiana Tech beat Alabama for the first time on November 1, 1997. At that point in the season, Tech was 6-2 overall and Alabama was 4-3. Tech scored first on a Marty Kent field goal and would continue to have the lead or at least be tied for the rest of the game. Sean Cangelosi, Josh Bradley and Troy Edwards all caught touchdown passes that day. Despite a few missed extra point attempts, Jeff Milonski added a field goal to round out the Bulldog win, 26–20. Quarterback Tim Rattay and company put up 522 yards of total offense on the Tide defense, while Alabama had 389 total offensive yards. It was Coach Gary Crowton's second year as Bulldog head coach, and his team would not lose another game that year, ultimately finishing 9-2. Alabama also did not win another game that year, finishing 4-7.

Ted Mandell published a book in 2006 called *Heartstoppers and Hail Marys: 100 of the Greatest College Football Finishes (1970–1999)*. It was, according to him, the one hundred greatest calls in college football history. Dave's honored to be in there somewhere. It's in chronological order at number ninety-eight. It was Saturday, September 18, 1999, a rematch with No. 18 Alabama, which Tech had beaten two years previously. The Jack Bicknell–coached Bulldogs were trailing 28–22 in the fourth quarter when Tim Rattay, the quarterback, was injured late in the game. He went limping badly to the sideline with a sprained right ankle, and Tech went to backup sophomore quarterback Brian Stallworth to replace him. Rattay had driven Tech down the field to the Alabama sixteen-yard line with only seconds left in the game when he was injured. Stallworth came on the field but was immediately sacked on his first play. With time running down, Stallworth ran back to the line, took the snap and hit wide receiver Sean Cangelosi in the end zone to tie the game. With the extra point by Kevin Pond, Tech won, 29–28. Dave almost screwed up the call when Stallworth hit Cangelosi. He said, "Touchdown, Bulldogs! You gotta love it!" The official, however, had not raised his

Dave Nitz, early 2000s. *From Dave Nitz.*

hands yet. They were SEC officials, to say the least. It took him about ten or fifteen seconds—he was looking around, probably wondering if he could throw a flag somewhere. But he didn't. The touchdown was good, and Tech won the game in front of eighty thousand people at Legion Field in Birmingham. That touchdown lives in infamy for Tech fans. It's on the disc of recorded calls in the book and a chapter for the Louisiana Tech–Alabama game.

MICHIGAN STATE FOOTBALL

In 2003, Tech brought down another giant. Coach Bicknell's team scored a couple of touchdowns in the last two minutes to win the game. Luke McCown was the quarterback and threw a couple of touchdowns in the last minute and fourteen seconds of the game to rally from a 19–7 deficit, beating Michigan State in East Lansing. It was quite an upset, and quite a win for Louisiana Tech, as it was Louisiana Tech University's first time to defeat a Big Ten school. Up until the last minute or so of the fourth quarter, Tech had only scored on a seventy-six-yard touchdown pass from

McCown to wide receiver Shawn Piper, with an extra point by Josh Scobee, which happened in the first quarter. The next Bulldog score occurred when McCown hit wide receiver Julius Cosby for a touchdown with 1:09 left in the game. The extra point was good, and the Bulldogs trailed 19–14 at that point. The only hope left was an onside kick, which somehow miraculously worked. McCown then drove the Bulldogs fifty-five yards down the field, ultimately connecting with wide receiver D.J. Curry on an eleven-yard touchdown, winning the game 20–19. To say the least, Michigan State has not invited Louisiana Tech back to play football any time recently—nor Alabama, for that matter.

SIOUX CITY EXPLORERS

Dave figured his baseball career was over after leaving the Sports. He talked with the president of the American Association, however, and reconsidered. They had clubs all over the Midwest. He said, "I understand Sioux City is looking for a play-by-play radio guy." *Oh, really?* Dave knew the general manager, Shane Tritz. They actually met several years ago when he was the manager of the Coastal Bend Aviators, and Dave was with the Sports. Their interview was his first as the home team manager. He didn't like how it went the first time, so they had to redo it, despite the two cracking up about it. One of them made a passing comment that maybe they would work together someday, and sure enough, they did. Dave called him: "Shane, I understand you're looking for a radio guy for next year."

He kind of chuckled. "Yeah, I am, you know of anybody?"

After he talked about what he had to offer, Dave said, "Okay, I'll tell you this: I've been burned one time on stuff like this, on verbal things. If you put all this in writing, send me a contract, and I'll sign it." Shane was going to furnish Dave a car, pay him so much for the year to do Sioux City Explorers baseball, put him up in a hotel (which became an apartment) in Sioux City and pay for the gas. When he sent the contract, Dave took the job. That was in 2008.

Shane was also one of the best general managers Dave had to work with. Dave asked him about his expectations. Just like Coach Lambright and Taylor Moore, he told Dave, "Do the job you're hired to do. If I was smart enough, I would do the job, but I can't. That's why I hired you." There a

Dave Nitz on the air with Louisiana Tech football coach Jack Bicknell, circa 2001. *From Dave Nitz.*

little bit of an age difference. Dave liked the nicknames that he was given, "Dr. Dave" and "Grandpa Dave." He learned that if you stick around long enough, you become the designated grandpa.

• • •

Dave worked up there in Sioux City for nine years and decided after the 2017 season that it might be time for a younger person to do it. As a matter of fact, some of the guys had a running joke. As the joke went, in a photograph of Babe Ruth calling his shot, Dave's the kid in the background pointing at him. Then, they asked Dave how it was watching Babe play during the Great Depression and so forth. Well, he's not quite that old—he was born a decade *after* all that! When Dave sent his note to the general manager, he sent a letter to the owner of the ball club about Dave leaving. He told the owner that it was good for Dave but bad for Sioux City. Dave appreciated that. They were good to him. He hopes that he was an asset for them in the nine years he was there. It was a lot of fun; he met some good people. He loves Sioux City in the Midwest and told them it was like a second home. He spent four months out of the year there over nine years, which is thirty-six months, about three years. Dave still misses them.

Looking back on it, Dave feels that he probably shouldn't have retired at that time because they treated him so well. In May 2022, the owner called him. "We have opening night on Tuesday, and we'd like for you to come up along with four other managers for opening night. You're the only broadcaster I want to come back. I want you to throw out the first pitch of the game." He flew Marlene and Dave up to Sioux City. It was a cold night in May, forty-something degrees. The owner said, "I know you are not used to this cold weather. Why don't you and your wife sit in my private suite during the game?" It was fun; they got to visit with fans. Dave was pleased for him to do that, the only broadcaster after his nine years there that they wanted back.

A West Virginia Reunion

Dave's been back home to West Virginia many times. One of the most important times was in 2014. Louisiana Tech was going to play at Marshall for the Conference USA championship. Dave had an accident when he stepped off the curb on the way to the stadium into a freezing puddle of water, soaking his foot. That might have been a portent of bad things to come because Tech lost the game.

Dave and some of his Tech broadcasting friends visited with some of his old classmates from Milton before the game. He revealed to his Tech friends that he had a numbers racket going on back in high school. The principal had gotten wind of it after a while and put a stop to it. It wasn't anything serious, just Dave with a sheet for the betting information and they would share a few coins on the winnings. When Dave met his old friends that morning, they wanted to know if he had brought the number sheet for the day. Everyone had a laugh about that. And no, he did not disappoint.

Dave also asked about Keith Morehouse, the son of Gene Morehouse, who was his mentor at WJLS in Beckley, West Virginia. Keith is a sportscaster at one of the TV stations in Huntington. One of the sportswriters at Marshall got them acquainted. Dave told Keith, "I just want to tell you how much I appreciated what your dad did for me. He sat down with a young guy, a whippersnapper who was wet behind the ears, and helped me out. He showed me the ropes of broadcasting."

Keith told him, "You're one of several people that have told me that, that he would help young people out." To this day, if a young person comes up to Dave and says, "Okay, Dave, help me out on this. What do I need to do?" Dave's going to help that young person out because he had somebody help him out when he was twenty years old. Pay it forward. Or if the broadcaster for the other team needed help with equipment malfunctions, he would help them out. That was Dave in a way paying back what Gene had done for him.

Unfortunately, as Dave puts it, a lot of young people nowadays think they're going to be on ESPN tomorrow. They don't want help. They think they know it all now. They don't ask as many questions as they used to. When he was just starting at WMMN in Fairmont, Dave was always bugging them, asking questions. He admits he was probably being a nuisance. Dave was just trying to find out everything he could about radio at that time. He doesn't see people doing that anymore. They think they know it all now. There's so many things that you can learn. Say you become the general manager at a radio station, and you've been a program director or you've written copy or you've done commercials. You've done news or sports. You know how to manage those people who are in those departments. If you haven't done any of that, what are you going to do? If they do something wrong or something you don't like, how do you correct them? You don't know how to correct them or the right way to go about it. But if you've worked in radio from the ground up, whether it's radio or journalism, it doesn't make a difference what it is. If you're driving a bus or a cab, if you don't know how to do those things from the ground up, you run into situations you're not familiar with. Dave still runs into things nowadays—he's been in radio for over sixty years—and wonders how he would have done this, because you never know what you're going to run into.

HELPING OUT THE YOUNG GUYS

One of the guys he helped out was former Louisiana Tech baseball player Steve Davison. Like many Tech fans from the mid-'70s and onward, Davison grew up listening to Dave Nitz Louisiana Tech broadcasts and his signature expression, "You gotta love it!" Davison's devotion to Nitz lasted beyond his Tech days; before joining him on the air, Davison

Left: Dave Nitz baseball card, Sioux City Explorers minor league baseball. *From Dave Nitz.*

Below: Dave Nitz and color commentator Steve Davison broadcasting a football game at Fresno State University. *Photo by Tom Morris.*

would call home while in law school and have his mother put the phone by the radio to listen to Nitz's broadcasts. Davison's thoughts sum up what so many others who have worked with Nitz over the years would say: "Joining him in the booth years later was a joy and privilege. I had no talent for radio play-by-play, but Dave carried me and made the experience enjoyable. I can't think of anyone more loved by a fanbase than Dave."

Kane McGuire was working in Louisiana Tech athletics. The men's basketball team was playing at Syracuse in 2014 when he decided to get him on the air. He was sitting beside Dave at the scorer's table with a headset, listening to him call the game while working on his laptop. Having twenty-one thousand people in the Carrier Dome makes it very loud, of course. Shortly before the end of the game, during a long timeout, Dave needed a way to fill the time. He turned and started talking to Kane, hoping that Kane would talk back to him. "Dave, I've never talked on the radio before," Kane protested, but Dave kept it up until he joined. Tech wound up losing by two, but Dave had gotten a new color broadcaster.

Another person he helped was Conner Ryan. At the time, Connor worked in tickets with Sioux City. They traded some play-by-play work in 2017. He wanted to impart to Connor that he needed to have his own style. Not that he had to go out of his way to be crazy or different to distinguish himself but that he needed his own voice. He shouldn't try to be Dave Nitz Jr. out there. Dave also made it clear that while you could be friendly toward players and joke with them, you couldn't *be* their friend. You had to keep it professional. There was one time that Conner had an issue with a player who was upset with him. Dave told him about similar issues he had had with players. It's going to happen, no matter what. There are many ways the players can get upset with you. It's part of the job, and you can't control it.

A LOUISIANA TECH HONOR

Having the Louisiana Tech home baseball radio booth named the Dave Nitz Radio Booth in 2021 was quite an unexpected honor for the veteran broadcaster. He had not thought it would happen again after the home radio booth for football was named for him in 2017. He was about to

Right: Dave Nitz, near the end of his broadcasting career. *From Dave Nitz.*

Below: Dave at the entrance to the baseball home radio booth named in his honor. *Photo by Tom Morris.*

Dave broadcasting in Louisiana Tech University's new baseball stadium. *Photo by Tom Morris.*

leave to watch some Sioux City baseball when Teddy Allen wanted him to tour the new press box the day before he left. The baseball facilities were one of several buildings on Tech's campus damaged by a tornado in 2019. When he got up that morning, Dave wasn't feeling well. He didn't know if he should stay and pack or see the press box. After thinking a little bit more, he decided to go and at least have lunch with Teddy. Broadcasters are good for a free lunch after all. He was not disappointed.

LOUISIANA TECH BASEBALL NOWADAYS

Dave likes the current Tech baseball coach. He thinks Lane Burroughs is one of the better coaches the university has had. He gets the most out of the players he has. He gets the bluebloods; he's not going to get the top recruits in the country, but he will get good players and mold them into better players. For example, they had four seniors drafted in the tenth round or better in the 2022 MLB Draft. That's the first time that's ever happened in Tech baseball history. LSU, which has always been a baseball powerhouse, also had four players drafted that year. That's saying something. A couple of the Tech guys were walk-ons. Lane saw them and asked them to walk on. One of them was Steele Netterville. He wasn't drafted because he decided to go to medical school. Dave asked

Top: Nitz and Allen broadcasting a football game at Mississippi State University. *Photo by Tom Morris*.

Bottom: Dave honored with Bulldog baseball jersey at final home regular season baseball game of his fiftieth year of broadcasting Louisiana Tech University athletics versus Western Kentucky University, flanked by President Jim Henderson and Athletic Director Ryan Ivey. *From Donny Crowe*.

him what he would do if he was drafted. He said, "I've already turned down med school one year to come back for my senior year of baseball. Being a doctor is going to be my career." Good for you, Steele. You know which way you're headed.

Dave is unsure if they'll get to go to Omaha, Nebraska, and the College World Series before he retires. He's hoping to get to broadcast a college world series game. The Bulldogs will have a long way to go and lots of bridges to cross before then—the future is being written. By the time of publication, the truth will come to pass regarding Tech's college world series fate.

Dave Nitz baseball card, Louisiana Tech University. *From Jan and Flint Sibayan.*

YOU GOTTA LOVE IT!

Dave gets that question all the time. When did you start that? He has no idea. Just a habit, no idea. It just came out one time and stuck. Other people most likely have said it. He can't remember anyone saying it for him to copy but remains sure other people have. It's one of those things when Tech has an exciting play, sometimes, it comes out. Sometimes, it doesn't. Doesn't make any difference what sport it is. It's not something that's planned. It could be compared to the adrenaline rush that generates a war cry.

SLOWING DOWN

By the time this book comes out, Dave will have retired from Louisiana Tech. It's been a mix of emotions. How can someone give something up that has become such a part of who they are? Dave has been broadcasting Tech baseball for fifty years, sixty-plus in total. He's come a long way from Spencer, West Virginia, in 1961 doing *Big Dave's Night Beat*. We all must slow down at some point, however. If he could, he would continue broadcasting until he's gone. Who know, maybe he'll broadcast somewhere else, although he doesn't know if anybody would hire him. He's in his eighties—most people are looking for somebody a little younger. However, he feels like he can still do it. He still feels like the voice is there; the drive is there to do baseball, wherever it may be, or other sports. So, he's not quite ready to give it up. We'll see what happens down the road. Whether it happens or not, broadcasting has been a good ride. At any rate, Louisiana Tech will be his legacy, and he can't think of many other places he would rather it have been.

CHAPTER 6

THE LITTLE THINGS

A s we near the end, Dave would want to mention a few of the things that have carried him through his broadcasting career. He didn't try to form an opinion when he broadcasted. He tried to tell people what was happening on the field or the court. Then they could make up their mind what they thought was going on. He didn't try to say, *boy, that guy screwed up there; you know, he threw that ball away*; and so forth. He didn't want to do that. One time with the Shreveport Captains, Dave was critical of a couple of players, and he found out quickly that he should gauge the situation a little more carefully. He never sugarcoated anything and had to go about his business realizing that that's part of it.

Dave had a boss in Oklahoma City who would not say anything negative when calling a game. He would say "short stop," or "that wasn't his fault," "that was a bad hop," something like that, because he knew the player's girlfriend, parents or wife was listening, and he didn't want to say anything bad about the player he was friends with. As Dave would say, you can't be that way in sports. You got to draw a line there. You're on this side of the line. You're broadcasting the game. They're on that side of the line; they're playing the game. You have to let people know what is happening on the field or on the basketball court. You've got to paint a picture. That's what he tried to do at J.C. Love Field for a fan listening for the first time. He would tell them, "We have the student apartments behind the left field fence, the railroad track that goes along the right field fence that people call the rally train or trees around the ballpark," little things like that. Paint a picture for the person who is listening to the game, so in their mind, they can actually see what's what.

That's one thing that has helped him through the years. Trying to paint a picture, not only of the game but of the surrounding area as well. People can't see it, but if you describe something to them, they can see it. If there's a porch down the left field line, only three hundred feet, you give them measurements of the baseball field. Then they realize that the ball could be hit out of there, because it's a fly ball to left field. The bullpens where the pitchers warm up, you tell them where it is. They can see that in their minds; they can see a pitcher warming up.

That's not to say that Dave wouldn't do his best to make interviews relaxing and comfortable for players, coaches and managers. He wanted to make sure that they could trust him. He wouldn't question a team's strategy. If there was a shift in defense against a hitter, it was probably because the hitter's bats broke 90 percent to the left. He might get in a jam at the plate and hit it to the right. If the ball was missed in the outfield, it wasn't for lack of a sound strategy.

You can't become emotionally involved in games either as a broadcaster. Dave advised a fellow broadcaster one time on this topic because sometimes his voice gave away that the home team was losing. Other times, you may hear announcers who are very big homers. You can tell when they are biased. Dave tried to keep an even keel. Then again, when it was a big moment, he would say, "You gotta love it!" Sometimes, he just couldn't help it.

On the Road (Again)

Dave has always liked to travel, in case you didn't notice. There were two truck stops he loved. One was Jubitz Truck Stop in Portland, Oregon. The other one was the I-80 Truck Stop in Iowa. It's the world's largest truck stop. Since he drove to most games, Dave was very excited any time they were heading to the Chicago area because that meant going to the I-80 Truck Stop. Shane Tritz commented one time that while most people would want to see Mount Rushmore and other historic sites, Dave wanted to go to the I-80 Truck Stop.

I mentioned the origin of the nickname "Freeway Dave," but really, Dave did the same thing pretty much anywhere he went. If he didn't drive there, he would rent a car and sightsee. Sam Wilkinson and Dave went on many of these trips together. They went to see the home of the Milwaukee Brewers, Milwaukee County Stadium. Bennie Thornell and Dave went to Yosemite and Lake Tahoe. They went to Major League games in the cities they were broadcasting before covering the games. Coach Patterson and Dave burned lots of rubber together. It was nothing for them to go to a Texas Rangers game from Ruston with some of the guys. Dave would drive to Arlington, and then they would watch the game before turning around and going back home. He never asked anyone to help him drive part of the way. He didn't mind it. He loved being on the road. Again.

Dave will continue to travel outside of broadcasting. He's been delivering rental cars for Enterprise part-time since 1998. He'll usually meet someone halfway and switch vehicles. Once, he flew to LaGuardia and picked up a Dodge Charger on Long Island. His son Jeff is a truck driver. Dave asked him about the best way to get out of New York without going through the city. Dave found out from the guy he picked up the car from that the route Jeff told him about was closed for construction work. "You're going to have to get on I-695, take the loop around, and go through downtown New York City." Going through New York at four o'clock on a Friday afternoon was not high on Dave's bucket list. On Park Avenue in Manhattan, the delivery trucks would just stop in the street because there was nowhere for them to park. He was sweating bullets, trying to avoid it. He finally called Jeff when he got to an open area. "How in the world do I get out of this mess?"

Jeff said, "Well, what do you see?"

"There's a sign here that says Lincoln Tunnel."

"Take the Lincoln Tunnel, keep going straight, and that'll take you to Interstate 95. That's where you need to go to get going south." Without Jeff, Dave thought he would still be stuck in downtown Manhattan. It was a nightmare.

• • •

Most of the time, Dave's driving by himself. Sometimes, he'll call Marlene to let her know where he is. It's a fun job. He likes it because he gets to meet different people. Dave's education has also been a journey. When he first started college, he was in business. He took two years of accounting. That was nothing but numbers, sitting at a desk, figuring. He thought, *Man, this is boring.* He ended up moving over to journalism. He finally got his degree in journalism at Louisiana Tech. That way, he got to meet people. That helped his career, too, as far as working in sports information and media relations on minor-league baseball teams. He had to write game notes every day. Had to deal with the press, get interviews from different players. Journalism helped Dave tremendously in his writing ability. Dave admits that he is not a natural-born writer. If you ask Keith Prince, he'd say, "What kind of a writer is Dave? If I had a red pen ready, I'm okay." Dave would write a story like he was on the radio. The scripts are a lot shorter because you usually only have thirty seconds. You have a page or two to write for a newspaper. Keith would tell him, "We need to have this a little longer." Dave would try to write a little longer, and Keith circled things—with a red pen.

Dave said, "Keith, you're going to run out of red pens before I graduate." He's just not much of a literature person. At Tech, he had to read *A Farewell to Arms*. He was not a fan of that.

Recently, Dave was listening to a talk show in Dallas that asked people, "if you had to do it over again, would you go into a different field?" One person called in and said they'd do the same thing. It was graphics or designing, something they wanted to do for life. There were a lot of people who said, "Nah, I've worked in this and that and I'd rather have done something else." As for Dave, the only thing he would have rather done, if he had been good enough, was play professional baseball. If he had played professional baseball, he speculates, he'd probably have wound up in Mexico, trying to make some money playing baseball as long as he could. Of course, probably not at his age, but that was always a desire of his. At first, he thought he could play pro basketball. After playing one year of college basketball, he decided that his basketball career wasn't going to go much further. Same thing with baseball. He did enjoy pitching batting practice in the minor leagues and at Tech for a little while when the NCAA allowed it. He had a batting cage at home and would throw in the backyard with Jeff and Jay. In other words, Dave was the pitching machine.

Food

Dave has gotten many comments on his food preferences. He likes food that is not too spicy. Some people may consider it plain in the South, especially in Louisiana. In fact, he's been accused of liking hospital food, but that's just the way he likes it. He likes to eat one part of his meal at a time. He doesn't usually mix his food together.

When it comes to drinks, Dave loves sweet tea. While at Sioux City, he went by McDonald's just about every day and got two sweet teas, one for himself and one for Shane Tritz. When it comes to soft drinks, he likes Dr Pepper and especially ginger ale; nothing beats Vernors Ginger Ale. John James Marshall, a sportswriter from Shreveport, was with him at the 1980 Women's Final Four in Mount Pleasant, Michigan, home of Central Michigan University. During some downtime, they went bowling. Dave was incredulous that there was no Vernors Ginger Ale to be had. He had to explain to John just how good it was, as he had never heard of it before. Vernors is the crème of the crop when it comes to ginger ale. It was founded in Detroit, but for some reason you couldn't find any in Mount Pleasant. When he's not eating fast food, Dave loves sauerkraut and hates spaghetti. When it was time for spring training in the minor leagues, there were so many great steakhouses, such as those that have been mentioned. When Jack Mull was the manager at the Shreveport Captains, he and Dave would order forty-ounce porterhouses each and go to town.

FAMILY

Dave has been fortunate to have such a great family. They have all supported him and his career. He's glad that his kids really got a kick out of their father being a broadcaster when they were young. They probably thought at times that he was a celebrity, but he didn't encourage it. He tried to be there for them as much as he could, but it was really hard with all the traveling he did. He was there for Jamie's graduation at Tech in 1986 and then immediately flew off to broadcast the next sporting event. Of course, that also happened to be his graduation from Tech as well. She followed in his footsteps to start an accounting degree, and like himself, she got out of accounting and finished in education.

Dave got Jamie, Jeff and Jay T-shirts from places he visited. Marlene might have rolled her eyes after a while because their wardrobes were dominated by college T-shirts. Jamie is a teacher, and both Jeff and Jay played sports and help Dave broadcast. He gets to live vicariously through Jeff since he's been driving trucks. Jay is assistant manager of a rehab clinic. Dave is really proud of all of them.

They've all been saints for putting up with him, but especially Marlene. She's been with him a long time, and he couldn't think of anyone else he'd

Dave congratulated by Louisiana Tech baseball team before his final regular season broadcast of Louisiana Tech athletics against Western Kentucky. *From Donny Crowe.*

have by his side. She keeps him honest and in line. She's told him before that there's not enough to write a book about and if there was, no one would read it! They've gone back and forth over that before, but it looks like Dave might have her beat this time.

Shortly before Jamie's daughter was born, they were thoughtful enough to clear it with Grandpa Dave that they would share a birthday. That was perhaps a little more thoughtful than the time that Jay interrupted Jamie's seventh birthday party.

A FEW ACCOMPLISHMENTS

Dave's not one to toot his own horn, but it is nice to receive recognition for services rendered. After all, he's proud to have earned them and represent the places he's worked at for so long. He never got to realize his dreams of playing or broadcasting at the Major League level, but has come to realize that this is about as good if not better.

Dave and Marlene, Jeff, Jay and Jamie at the President's House at Louisiana Tech University. *From Dave Nitz.*

In 2009, Dave was named Louisiana Sportscaster of the Year. For several years, he was named the College Broadcaster of the Year by the Louisiana Sportswriters Association. In 2010, he entered the Louisiana Tech Sports Hall of Fame. Finally, in 2019, he entered the Louisiana Sports Hall of Fame.

The Future

Dave doesn't know exactly what he will be doing after retiring from Louisiana Tech. He's talked about possible adventures into broadcasting elsewhere and traveling. We'll see. He'll still be cutting his grass. He's very particular about it. If he could, he would stripe his yard baseball style. In his childhood, Dave pushed a propellor lawn mower at the house on Saunders Creek. Unsurprisingly, once he moved off to college, his father purchased a power lawn mower.

The real elephant in the room is broadcasting. Unfortunately, Dave doesn't make a good fan. He can't stand to sit there and watch a game. He feels like he must be doing something. He might wind up doing it somewhere else if they'll have him. It's like legendary announcer Harry Caray once said, "Drag me out of the press box feet first. That would be the best way to go."

No matter what happens, Dave will always be grateful for the friends he's made at Louisiana Tech University, the great people he has worked with and the truly loyal fans who have listened to him be the voice of the Bulldogs for so long. He can only sum it up by saying, "You gotta love it!" For now, good night to Marlene, Jamie, Jeff, Jay and their dog Jingles. So long everybody.

Top: Dan Newman and Lieutenant Governor Billy Nungesser presenting Dave Nitz with his Louisiana Sports Hall of Fame Trophy. *Photo by Tom Morris.*

Bottom: Dave speaking during the festivities of the Louisiana Sports Hall of Fame Class of 2019 induction ceremony. *Photo by Tom Morris.*

Clockwise from top left: Dave Nitz visiting with fellow Class of 2019 inductee, football legend Peyton Manning. *Photo by Tom Morris.*

Dave Nitz shaking Manning's hand on stage beside class of 2019 inductee, basketball legend Charles Smith. *Photo by Tom Morris.*

Dave's HOF trophy. *Photo by Tom Morris.*

Top: Dave broadcasting a Louisiana Tech basketball game from the 2020–21 season. *From Dave Nitz.*

Bottom: Dave Nitz and color commentator Jack Thigpen broadcasting a basketball game at the Thomas Assembly Center. *Photo by Tom Morris.*

Top: Dave Nitz and class of 2019 inductee, rodeo legend T. Berry Porter. *Photo by Tom Morris*.

Bottom: Dave Nitz and Kelvin "Kelbo" Lewis at the 1984–85 Louisiana Tech basketball Reunion. *From Dave Nitz*.

Dave with his headset in the baseball booth. *Photo by Tom Morris.*

An intense Dave broadcasting a basketball game. *Photo by Tom Morris.*

Dave Nitz on the air with Louisiana Tech basketball coach Eric Konkol. *Photo by Tom Morris.*

Dave Nitz on the air with Louisiana Tech football coach Skip Holtz. *Photo by Tom Morris.*

Dave enjoying a broadcast at a Sioux City Explorers game. *Photo by Tom Morris.*

EPILOGUE

The following is a special contribution by Jennifer Nitz, Dave's daughter-in-law.

The phrase "Life is a funny old dog" has been attributed to A.A. Milne, known for his Winnie the Pooh stories. Milne understood life in a way that many philosophers just don't seem to get—life is best experienced, not explained. Perspective often closes the circle.

When I joined the Dave Nitz family in 1996 with the selfishness that is often seen in youth, I thought I was gaining a last name that was closer to the front of the line and much, much shorter than the name I had grown up with (Shoalmire). I was already teaching, and my biggest challenge was getting my students to call me by my married name. When Jay and I were dating, we often went to sports events—nothing goes better with fun than free. Jay would take me to the radio booth to see his dad, but I had no idea who Dave Nitz really was. After almost thirty years, I am continually amazed by who Dave Nitz is.

History is one of my favorite subjects, and that includes listening to personal histories from different people. I've always been a listener; I like to ask people questions about their life, and I like to hear their stories. And I have heard some stories from Dave. And now, you've heard them, too. From his early stories about broadcasting from a library to later stories about how he got his nickname "Freeway Dave," to all of the names that he has called out for Louisiana Tech that made it to the "bigs," I have enjoyed hearing Dave's stories. But even more, I've enjoyed becoming a

Above: Louisiana Tech baseball coach Lane Burroughs interviewed by Dave Nitz. *Photo by Tom Morris.*

Opposite: Dave Nitz baseball card, Louisiana Tech University. *From Louisiana Tech University Athletics.*

part of his stories. Our family visited Dave and enjoyed Louisiana Tech games all over. I've listened to Dave from all over the United States, as we have traveled. Wherever we went, we were able to "see" the games as Dave drew pictures with his words of the game and the players. Two of the most memorable events were listening to father and son co-broadcast Louisiana Tech baseball games and attending Dave's induction into the Louisiana Sports Hall of Fame.

As a former English teacher and now a librarian, I have heard and read a lot of stories. There are basics to any story: a plot, a setting, characters, point of view and conflict. Dave's story has lots of settings, characters, conflicts, and even points of view but only one plot: the events that shaped Dave's life. And these events have created a life story that is so interesting that he had to share it. Ira Glass said, "Great stories happen to those who can tell them." If that is the case, then Dave Nitz has told a great story, in a life he has experienced. And the circle closes, not ending but complete.

ABOUT THE AUTHOR

Christopher Alan Kennedy is a historian who loves learning about his home state, Louisiana. His first book, *Louisiana Tech's Joe Aillet*, published by The History Press in 2022, is a biography of the namesake of Louisiana Tech University's football stadium. A 2023 LSU graduate with an MLIS and two-time Tech alumnus, he was part of a team that cataloged museum items at the USS Kidd Veterans Museum and removed items from the destroyer to prepare for the ship's departure for renovations at a Gulf Coast drydock. When he's not working, he's most likely running, hiking, hanging out with friends and family or getting ready for fantasy football or March Madness.